Making Chocolates

Making Chocolates

Alec Leaver

Weathervane Books • New York

Copyright © MCMLXXV by Alec Leaver
Library of Congress Catalog Card Number: 76-53668
This edition is published by Weathervane Books
a division of Imprint Society, distributed by Crown Publishers, Inc.
by arrangement with Michael Joseph Ltd.

a b c d e f g h

Contents

List of Illustrations

Acknowledgements

It surely cannot be entirely coincidence that when those gentle and peaceful people, the Quakers, were first being persecuted by their fellow Christians, and prevented from entering the professions, a number sought refuge in sweet and chocolate making. So the great names of Rowntree, Fry and Cadbury became known throughout the world, not only as chocolate and cocoa manufacturers, but as public benefactors in many fields. Perhaps if more people made chocolates there might, just possibly, be less violence, not only of the sort used by one individual against another, but that of the state against the individual as well as the massive incomprehensible destruction of which modern industrial nations are capable.

Many people helped in the making of this book, consciously or not, including Margaret Batey, Ginette Richard, Margaret Bain, Mandy Bateman, Joanne Montgomery, Sheila Houghton, Ann Craven, Jimpy Mendham and Norman Hamilton. I had considerable help from members of the staff of Westminster Technical College, especially Mr Griggs and Mr Rolfe. Lastly, my parents, particularly mother who is, among many other things, a superb cook.

Introduction

Making chocolates is a most exciting and delightful branch of cookery. It gives enormous scope to anyone with imagination and artistic flair, but superb results can be achieved simply by reproducing the kind of chocolates which are available in commercially-made assortments. Home-made chocolates are much superior to the normal commercial product, partly because you can use better quality ingredients giving improved flavour or texture, even though they may be more expensive or likely to deteriorate more quickly, and partly because you can choose your own centres and make those which you particularly like.

Experience in making chocolates also helps towards an understanding of the chocolatier's art and an appreciation of really well-made chocolates. Fortunately, many of the problems which the manufacturer has to solve need not worry the home chocolatier. He has to be concerned with, among other things, costing, quality control and uniformity of batches, stock control and storage conditions. On the other hand, he is able to obtain some equipment and materials not available in the shops, whereas the home chocolatier has to adapt available equipment and occasionally may have to make extra utensils. None of this is beyond any handyman or woman and detailed instructions will be given when necessary; but it is very important to use the right equipment even if it must be bought. It can waste so much time and materials if you attempt to work with the wrong tools.

The manufacturer also employs craftsmen with years of experience and enormous skill, who cannot be emulated in minutes, but they have to work at very great speed, often looking after many processes at once. The home chocolatier can take things much more slowly, and with a little practice only an expert will be able to tell that your chocolates are made at home rather than purchased from some fabulously expensive shop.

Making chocolates certainly requires a great deal of patience and a capacity to take considerable pains, but many other hobbies require no less. Some of the quantities in the recipes have to be measured exactly. Whereas in other forms of cooking, a recipe calling for, say 2 oz. of an ingredient will probably not be much affected if you put in 3 oz. instead; in chocolate-making it might spell ruin. However, even in home carpentry a miscalculation of $\frac{1}{8}$ in. can spoil a piece of woodwork, so quite a high level of accuracy is required in that craft too. I will try to indicate which quantities are critical and which can be altered without affecting the result. In a number of ways, making chocolates differs from other aspects of cookery and a good knowledge of cooking may not always be an advantage here. For instance, the longer meat and vegetables are cooked, the more tender they become, as a rule. Not so with sugar, the most important ingredient in chocolate centres: the longer sugar is cooked, the harder it becomes. So one of the basic principles that every housewife accepts, almost without thinking, is completely reversed in chocolate-making.

I think the best way to approach the making of chocolates is to regard it as something entirely new that you must learn about right from the beginning. Otherwise, you may find some of the recipes extremely odd, feel you ought to do them the way your experience says you should, and end up with a mess. On the other hand, don't be too nervous. If anything goes wrong, it is quite likely the ingredients need not be wasted but can be used again. At worst, the main ingredient of most centres, sugar, is fairly cheap and it is no great expense to throw some away. The important thing is to make an attempt, following the instructions as exactly as you can, and see what happens. You will probably feel that there are far too many things to be done all at once, but all you need is a little practice, so have a shot, and when you understand the process completely you can then start experimenting for yourself.

Of course, the great trick is coating the centres with chocolate, since once you can do that you can coat almost anything even if it is not up to standard – that is, provided the centre is thick enough just to hold its shape. Making chocolates look exciting on the surface is a very important part of making them taste delicious.

As your skill increases and becomes known among your acquaintances, you can develop a lucrative little hobby since many people will be willing to buy your products, and their friends will bring in new business. A very few professional chocolatiers still make chocolates, more or less as a home industry. Mr and Mrs Avison have a tiny shop in Preston Road, Brighton. Mrs Avison comes from a family of Belgian chocolatiers and she and her husband make their chocolates in the evening and sell them fresh next day. It is a pity their work is not more widely appreciated and that they have not more scope to use their skill and ability; but it does illustrate that making chocolates at home can even be done on a commercial basis. It is important, however, not to sell too cheaply. Prices should cover time, knowledge and experience, not just materials and overheads.

Chocolates make very acceptable gifts for birthdays or at Christmas. I even give occasional boxes as wedding presents and none of the happy couples has complained yet. Charities are pleased to accept chocolates for their bring and buy sales or bazaars. There are many ways in which this unusual skill can give a lot of pleasure to others as well as to yourself.

This book is not a collection of recipes which can be looked up and just made straight away: it would be a waste of time for any beginner to attempt to work from a book of that sort. Rather, it attempts to take the reader step by step through the various processes of making chocolates, starting with the easiest one, the truffle, so that one can see how all the various types of centre are related.

By the end of the book, you will understand all the basic characteristics of a wide range of chocolate centres and have practised all the more important techniques used in chocolate-making. Then you will be able to make all sorts of chocolates and, moreover, be able to start inventing your own without any risk of mistakes.

The best plan would be to read the book chapter by chapter. After studying this next chapter, you should make at least a few truffles, which will give valuable experience in handling chocolate, so that the subsequent chapter on chocolate preparation and dipping will be much easier to understand. Similarly, you should understand the chapter on sugar-boiling before trying to make caramels. Fudge is the next step and it will be found much easier to make if you have already tried the caramels in the earlier chapter. Tackled in this way, the whole picture will become clear and you will gradually become very proficient without making too many mistakes through lack of adequate background knowledge.

I have usually described every process thoroughly once only. When any process is referred to in a later recipe, I have normally given only a brief summary rather than the full details in order to save space and prevent tedious repetition. I apologise in advance to anyone who would have preferred it the other way.

A word about ingredients. There is no point in paying more than you need for materials you use in large quantities. Before buying, say chocolate for truffles, or cornflour for a starch tray, compare prices at all your local stores, you will find some surprising differences and you can make some useful savings.

Lastly, a note about measures. A pint of water weighs 1 lb. 4 oz., or 20 oz. Therefore, a container which can hold a pint is said to have a capacity of 20 fl. oz. (fluid ounces), and a quarter-pint or gill equals 5 fl. oz. Tablespoons and teaspoons are not very accurate measures and are best avoided. In fact, 3 slightly overflowing tablespoonfuls, or 3 level tablespoonfuls one tea-spoonful, equal 2 fl. oz., so cutlery is awkward as well as inaccurate. Where recipes do suggest them, it is best to use a set of proper measuring spoons. The best measure for small quantities of liquid is a small glass measuring jar used by chemists. These can sometimes be bought quite cheaply second-hand, sometimes even stamped for accuracy by the Weights and Measures inspector. A measure which ranges up to 2 or 4 fl. oz. would be extremely useful for making truffles.

All the quantities in the recipes are given in ounces and pints and the temperatures in Fahrenheit.

I

Truffles

Truffles are the easiest chocolates to make and certainly the most delightful to eat. They provide an excellent introduction to the problems of handling and coating centres which are very important in chocolate-making.

The basis of the truffle centre is ganache paste, a mixture of melted chocolate and warm cream well blended and cooled until it hardens. Orange, honey, peppermint, rum or vanilla can be added to give flavour, but it is important that the final mixture should be hard enough to be moulded to shape and be capable of standing up to being coated with chocolate.

The texture of ganache paste depends upon the kinds of cream and chocolate and the proportions in which they are used. Plain chocolate is harder than milk chocolate, so more cream can be added to it. Single cream is thinner than double so must be used in smaller quantities. Using double cream and a plain chocolate such as Bourneville, $\frac{1}{2}$ pint or 10 fl. oz. of cream to 1 lb. of chocolate will give a firm consistency. Using 'whipping cream', which can be made by mixing single cream with a little more than the same quantity of double cream, 1 lb. milk chocolate such as Cadbury's Dairy Milk should be mixed with not more than 6 fl. oz. (just over $\frac{1}{4}$ pint). Sterilised cream in tins can be used, but it is only slightly thicker than single cream and is much too thin to use instead of double cream. The amounts of cream must be reduced when other liquids are added for flavouring.

Incorporating cream or other liquids fulfils two functions: it softens the chocolate and it gives flavour. Any liquid can be added to chocolate and will have a softening effect, if that is all that is required. Even water can be used, although its effect is so drastic that the quantity must be very accurate indeed: 3 fl. oz. of water added to 1 lb. milk chocolate gives a slightly soft consistency 4 fl. oz. would make it much too soft, while only 2 fl. oz. would leave it too hard to mould. It is important to be as accurate as possible, even when using cream, but there is room for a little error.

After the centre has been made and moulded to shape, it is coated with chocolate to seal it and help to keep it moist. It is then rolled in a final decorative coating, and this can be cocoa sweetened with a little icing sugar, chocolate sugar strands, grated chocolate, nib almonds or chopped mixed nuts. This centre does not keep for more than a week or two in warm weather since it is subject to mould, so it is wise to store truffles in the refrigerator. They can be kept in the deep freeze in a sealed container, but when the centres are very cold they have no flavour and should be brought to room temperature slowly. Remove them from the freezer a day before you need them, keeping the container closed to prevent condensation forming on the chocolates as they warm up.

The recipe for Vanilla Truffles gives the basic method of making truffles in detail. The other kinds of truffle involve only simple variations on this method, therefore only a brief summary of the method is given with the other recipes.

Vanilla Truffles

Equipment: Double-boiler or pudding bowl in a pan, pastry-board or plate, small saucepan, tablespoon, two teaspoons, wooden spoon, electric mixer (optional).

Ingredients: ½ lb. 'Dairy Milk' chocolate or 'Galaxy'

3 fl. oz. Whipping cream ($1\frac{1}{4}$ fl. oz. single and
$1\frac{3}{4}$ fl. oz. double cream – say $1\frac{3}{4}$ tablespoonfuls
to $2\frac{3}{4}$ tablespoonfuls; alternatively, it can be
weighed out, reckon 1 fl. oz.$=$1 oz.)
vanilla essence
4 level tablespoonfuls cocoa and one of icing
sugar, sieved together.

Method: Break up the chocolate and put it into a basin or
double-boiler. Put the basin in hand-hot water not exceeding
125°F. If using a double-boiler or a basin in a pan where the
water does not reach the basin, put enough water in the base,
heat until large bubbles start to rise to the surface (the temperature will be about 160°F.), remove from the heat and place the
basin over the hot water. Stir the chocolate occasionally until
thoroughly melted. Bring the cream to the boil to sterilise it,
then cool to hand-hot. Add a few drops of vanilla essence, then
tip it into the melted chocolate and stir until it is all thoroughly
mixed.

Chocolate should never be heated above 120°F. even after
the cream has been added, or the fat may separate, leaving a
brown rubbery mass. It is possible to save it by cooling and beating, but the texture will never be the same and a lot of flavour
is lost.

The mixture should be allowed to cool to normal room temperature – about 65°F. – stirring occasionally to equalise the
temperature of the mixture. The paste will now be quite thick
but not hard.

Stir with the wooden spoon, or if possible beat with an electric
mixer, until the mixture is lighter in colour and fluffy. This
process is very important to give the right texture. Allow to
cool again, preferably in a refrigerator until the mixture hardens.
A refrigerator is very useful for chilling truffle paste quickly, and
in summer the temperatures may be so high as to make it
essential.

Dust a board with sieved sweetened cocoa and with two teaspoons measure out roughly enough of the paste to make into balls $\frac{3}{4}$ to $\frac{7}{8}$ in. in diameter. Drop the rough lumps at intervals on the board until you have used all the paste. Then, dipping the fingers in the sweetened cocoa, pick up the pieces and quickly press them into balls, replacing them on the cocoa-covered board before the paste melts and they become sticky. Use as little cocoa as possible or it may thicken the chocolate when the centres are being coated. You could use sieved icing sugar for this operation except that it does not improve the appearance of the chocolate and can be mistaken for mould when you bite into it.

The centres can be put back in a cool place or in the 'fridge for a short time to chill and firm the outside. If the mixture is very moist, the centres can be kept a day or so until the outside has dried and a little crust has formed. It is then much easier to handle.

COATING TRUFFLES

Equipment: Double-boiler or pudding-bowl in a pan, pastry-board or plate, one extra plate, two teaspoons and an eye-dropper from the chemist.

Ingredients: $\frac{1}{2}$ lb. plain chocolate
4 level tablespoonfuls of cocoa and one of icing sugar sieved together
a few drops of glycerine (optional)
1–2 tablespoons of vegetable oil or fat.

Method: Melt the chocolate in the double-boiler or basin in hot water. Do not heat above 120°F. but make sure it is thoroughly melted, stirring frequently. Mix the sieved cocoa and icing sugar and spread it out in a layer on the plate or board. When the chocolate is thoroughly melted, remove it from the water, carefully drying underneath the container so that no drips accidentally splash on the centres. Check the temperature and consistency of the chocolate by pouring about a teaspoonful on the fingers of the left hand. By working the chocolate between the fingers and thumb it will cool to lukewarm and it should be thick enough to give a reasonable depth of coating but not so thick that it begins to feel rubbery. Eating chocolate seems to vary in consistency from time to time and it is very difficult to give precise instructions to achieve exactly the right consistency. Experience is the best guide.

If the chocolate appears too thin, add two or three drops of water or glycerine, measuring carefully with an eye-dropper, and stir. The chocolate will thicken or 'tighten' which is the way confectioners prepare chocolate for piping. In hot weather, even moisture from your fingers may thicken the chocolate. When you are using glycerine, the chocolate will have to be stirred for $1-1\frac{1}{2}$ minutes before it thickens, but it sets with a much better gloss. However, this is not so important for our present purpose.

If the chocolate is too thick, stir in any tasteless vegetable oil or fat such as Trex or Spry, trying half a teaspoonful first, then perhaps a little more.

Now all is ready for finishing the chocolates. Set everything out on a table ready to hand. If you are right-handed, have the plate of centres on your right, the bowl of thickened chocolate in front and the plate of cocoa mixture on the left with another plate or tray on which the finished truffles can be placed. Spread some of the chocolate on the fingers of the left hand, roll it round the fingers and thumb until the chocolate feels quite cool. Place a centre on the fingers, pour about half a teaspoonful of chocolate over it and roll it about until it is thoroughly coated with a layer of chocolate between $\frac{1}{16}$ in. and $\frac{1}{8}$ in. thick. Then place it on the layer of cocoa, sprinkle some over the surface of the chocolate and roll the centre over the cocoa until it has just picked up enough to cover. Allow the coating to set hard before transferring it to another clean plate or tray.

If the chocolate is too warm or has not been thickened enough, you may have to coat several centres and place them on the cocoa before starting to roll them, otherwise they may pick up too much cocoa and form a very deep coating. The object is to have the chocolate as cool as possible and therefore as near setting point as possible, but not so cool that it sets before it can be coated with cocoa. Sometimes you will notice patches of chocolate not covered with cocoa, which set quite glossy instead of dull or streaky. This is because the chocolate has been 'tempered' and tempering is extremely important in making chocolates. The next chapter shows in greater detail how this is done.

The most frequent faults in truffles are cracks and pinholes in the chocolate coating. In the case of pinholes, the centre spurts out like a little piece of string. Both faults arise from the same cause: when chocolate is warmed, it expands; when it is cooled, it contracts. If the centre is too cold when the chocolate is applied and it is then left in a normal room temperature of 60–65°F., the centre will warm up and expand while the coating is cooling down and contracting. The result is a build-up of pressure inside the chocolate which either cracks the coating or, if there is a weak spot such as an air-bubble, it makes a little hole and forces some of the soft centre through it. The best cure is prevention, by allowing the centre to remain in the 'fridge, before coating, for just long enough to chill the outside, while the inner part remains at room temperature. The centre can also be kept in the hand a little longer while it is being coated with chocolate, as this helps to warm it above room temperature so that it cools and contracts with the coating.

It is easier for two to carry out this operation, one person coating the centres with chocolate while the other coats with cocoa, but it is perfectly possible to do it alone. It is much less complicated than it sounds, the important thing is to give it a trial. If the first chocolates turn out less than perfect, you can always eat them yourself.

Now some variations on the basic Vanilla Truffle recipe.

*   *   *

Truffles

Orange Truffles

Equipment: As for Vanilla Truffles.

Ingredients: ½ lb. dark chocolate such as 'Bourneville'
4 fl. oz. double cream (6 standard tablespoonfuls)
concentrated orange
2 oz. almonds or mixed nuts.

Method: Melt the chocolate as described for Vanilla Truffles.
Bring the cream to the boil to sterilise it before adding it, cooled,
to the chocolate. Stir to mix properly and add enough concentrated orange juice to give a good flavour. 'Sunquick' make a
concentrated orange which gives a nice bite. Try one tablespoonful and add another half if required. Two teaspoonfuls or
so of grated orange rind added to the cream before heating also
helps to improve the flavour.

Stir the mixture well, using a beater if you have one. Allow
the mixture to cool to between 60 and 65°F., then stir again
until it creams and becomes lighter in colour and texture. Put
aside to cool again and set. Form into balls and coat with melted
chocolate as described earlier. Finally, roll in nib almonds
(almonds chopped to a maximum size of ⅛ in. square) or you can
use chopped mixed nuts which may, if you wish, be roasted in
the oven beforehand at a temperature of 290–310°F.

Honey Truffles

Equipment: As for Vanilla Truffles.

Ingredients: 5 oz. milk chocolate
2 oz. honey (hard not clear)
5 oz. plain chocolate
4 fl. oz. double cream.

Method: Melt the chocolate and add the warmed cream as
described previously. The ½-lb. blocks of 'Dairy Milk' and
'Bourneville' are conveniently moulded into ¼-oz. divisions with
four to a row, so it is not necessary to weigh it. Mix in the

honey, beat well and allow to cool. When the mixture is sufficiently cool, stir or whisk to cream it and then allow it to set.
Roll out the mixture into long ropes $\frac{1}{2}$ to $\frac{5}{8}$ in. in diameter
using about a third at a time, on a board covered with sieved
sweetened cocoa. Cut off pieces $1\frac{1}{4}$ to $1\frac{1}{2}$ in. long and allow the
surface to dry out or chill in the refrigerator for a short time.
Coat in the usual way with melted chocolate and finish in cocoa.
If you wish to use clear honey, use less cream or the mixture
will be too soft.

Coffee Truffles

Equipment: As for Vanilla Truffles.

Ingredients: 5 oz. milk chocolate
5 oz. plain chocolate
$\frac{1}{4}$ pint (5 fl. oz.) double cream
4 teaspoonfuls instant coffee or liquid concentrate
8 oz. chocolate sugar strands.

Method: Melt the chocolate. Sterilise the cream and allow it
to cool. Stir the coffee into the cream and add it to the chocolate.
If using a liquid concentrated coffee such as 'Camp', use only 4
fl. oz. cream or the mixture may be a little too soft. Mix
thoroughly, cool, stir and allow to set in the usual way, then
roll out and make little sausage shapes as for Honey Truffles.
Coat these in chocolate but this time finish them by rolling in
the sugar strands.

Rum Truffles

Equipment: As for Vanilla Truffles.

Ingredients: 9 oz. plain chocolate
4 fl. oz. double cream
1 fl. oz. rum ($1\frac{1}{2}$ tablespoonfuls)
8 oz. chocolate sugar strands.

Method: Make the paste as described for Vanilla Truffles,
adding the rum to the chocolate after the cream. If rum is heated

too much, it loses flavour. You could use 2 tablespoonfuls of rum if you like it stronger, but the rum and cream together should total a little under 5 fl. oz. or ¼ pint. This mixture will seem very thin when warm but it will thicken quite satisfactorily as it cools. Rum Truffles are usually shaped into balls before being coated in chocolate and finished in chocolate sugar strands.

Peppermint Truffles

Make a paste in exactly the same way as for Vanilla Truffles but instead of using vanilla essence, use peppermint oil. This can be purchased from chemists; it is very expensive but has a much better flavour than cheaper substitutes. It should be added very gradually with an eye-dropper, and 5 to 10 drops should be enough. These centres can also be shaped into balls, coated in chocolate and rolled in grated chocolate. To grate chocolate, use the coarse grater; you can get quite long flakes if the chocolate is not too cold.

From these basic recipes you can carry out your own experiments with different flavours using, perhaps, liqueurs or other spirits instead of rum, or mixing in chopped or ground nuts, glacé or maraschino cherries or chopped crystallised or preserved ginger. With maraschino cherries and preserved ginger, make sure they are thoroughly dried before being added to the paste.

You can, of course, use your own choice of chocolate for the paste. If you prefer milk chocolate in the Orange Truffles or all plain chocolate in the Coffee Truffles, all you need to remember is that milk chocolate gives a softer mixture and therefore you must use less cream to compensate. If the paste turns out to be very soft, it can be warmed again so that more melted chocolate can be added, or while still cool it can be thickened by folding in sieved cocoa and icing sugar.

Truffle centres are made from many other ingredients such as evaporated or condensed milk, butter, margarine or vegetable oils instead of cream, and every manufacturer has his own recipe. You can add an ounce or so of butter or margarine to one of the recipes to try it out. Vegetable oils and fats, however, have no flavour and do nothing to improve truffles. Icing sugar and fondant, which we shall be making later, are also used, partly as sweeteners, partly to give a crystalline texture.

The finish of truffles is a matter of choice. The two shapes described earlier are round balls and sausage shapes, but a drum shape is also quite simple to make. Squares and oblongs are more difficult to handle and most chocolate makers tend to reserve them for harder centres such as caramels, fudges and nougats. The finishes consisted of sweetened cocoa, chopped nuts, chocolate sugar strands and grated chocolate. You may be able to experiment with other coatings.

The object is to give each chocolate with a different type of centre its own attractive and distinctive appearance so that one can tell what the centre is. A box of four or five different kinds of truffles is attractive to the eye and delightful to eat. Alternatively, a few truffles with their different finishes and shapes can be used in a box with other chocolates to give it variety and interest.

2

Chocolate Preparation and Dipping

Chocolate is a carefully processed product consisting of cocoa butter (a hard, almost brittle fat) and a brown finely ground powder, both of which are derived from the seeds of the cacao tree, to which sugar may be added for the purpose of sweetening. The brown particles do not dissolve in the cocoa butter but remain suspended in it. This fact is of great importance in using chocolate, since it means that when chocolate is in a molten state the cocoa butter can separate from the brown particles. The particles, being heavier, tend to sink, and the chocolate when it cools may set with a whitish surface, which is the separated cocoa butter. This is less of a problem when the cocoa butter content is low. The process of 'tempering' chocolate is necessary to overcome this tendency, so that a chocolate with a high cocoa butter content can be made to set with a glossy brown surface and no evidence of white blotches or streaks.

TYPES OF CHOCOLATE

There are three kinds of chocolate for three different purposes: eating, baking and coating. Eating chocolate contains a moderate amount of cocoa butter. When melted, it is relatively very thick; and when allowed to set, the surface becomes rather dull. A better finish can be achieved by casting the chocolate in polished moulds; the front of a bar of chocolate, where the divisions are

27

imprinted by a mould, is always glossier than the back for this reason.

Baking chocolate has a much softer consistency as a rule, achieved by replacing a high proportion of the cocoa butter with softer vegetable fats. Mainly used for decoration in confectionery, a coating of this kind will cut easily without shattering – important on a cake which is to be cut into portions. However, it is greasy to the touch and has very little flavour although greatly improved baking chocolates are now being made. Their real advantage is that they set with a reasonable gloss without having to be tempered.

Coating chocolate, or 'couverture' as it is usually called, is used primarily for coating chocolates and biscuits and contains a high proportion of cocoa butter. This means it must be tempered properly: when it is, couverture has a glossy finish, a good hard 'snap' and therefore does not feel greasy, and excellent flavour. These are the three characteristics which distinguish couverture from the other types of chocolate.

Milk chocolate is simply a flavour obtained by adding milk solids and butter fat to chocolate. Other flavours which may be added to eating chocolate include coffee, orange and peppermint.

Therefore, baking chocolate is unsuitable for coating chocolates since it is too soft and lacks flavour, while eating chocolate could be used if it were thinned down with extra cocoa butter. Unfortunately, this is expensive and difficult to obtain. Chemists may be able to obtain it; they call it Oil of Theobroma and used to make suppositories with it. To make chocolates comparable with the best professional products, it is necessary to use real couverture for which you will need to find a supplier.

Some manufacturers of couverture will only supply the trade. Others will supply members of the public, but their machines automatically make and pack 28 lb. or 56 lb. at a time and they are reluctant to break open boxes to sell in smaller quantities. It is normally made in 7-lb. or 10-lb. blocks, the larger ones measuring about 9 x 19 in. and $1\frac{1}{4}$ in. thick. One block is not too much to start with since it keeps in perfect condition for months if stored below 70°F. Bakers' and confectioners' wholesalers may be prepared to help, but again many of these only supply the trade. It would be worth approaching a local baker or confectioner who, if he does not use couverture himself, could obtain it for you, although my experience in the London area is that they are not very helpful. A grocer's or delicatessen may occasionally stock couverture, but they sometimes think baking chocolate is the same thing and try to sell you that instead. The most likely source is a hand-made chocolate shop or small chocolate factory. If there is such a place locally it is well worth getting in touch, for apart from supplying chocolate, the proprietor will have a real interest in his craft and, like all craftsmen, want to be helpful to beginners. A conducted tour of the factory would be a fascinating and invaluable experience from which much useful information could be gathered.

I have obtained couverture in the London area from: The House of Floris, 39 Brewer Street, London, W.1; Junelle's Chocolates, 16 High Street, Wimbledon, London, S.W.19; T. C. Ford & Sons, The Subway, Clapham Junction Station, London, S.W.11 (milk chocolate only).

TEMPERING CHOCOLATE

Put simply, tempering couverture is a process of warming it until it is thoroughly melted and can be properly mixed, cooling it until it thickens and is almost at setting-point, and finally warming it until it is just thin enough to use but still thick enough to set very quickly, before the cocoa butter has time to rise to the surface. Frequent stirring is essential at all stages to keep the cocoa particles well distributed throughout the cocoa butter.

Neither the cocoa particles nor the sugar actually affects the process of tempering, which is necessary because of the peculiar nature of cocoa butter. This is, in fact, a complex of fats, each of which melts and sets at a different temperature. However, even the hardest melts before 98.4°F. normal body temperature; if it did not, it could not melt in the mouth and would stick to the teeth like the very hard fats used in some manufactured puff pastries. To ensure that chocolate is fully melted, it is usual to warm it to a somewhat higher temperature, over 110°F. and to do it gradually, stirring frequently to equalise the heat. But chocolate must never be heated beyond 120°F. or the flavour and gloss will be diminished and the final result look less professional. It may even become lumpy.

When the couverture is cooled, to about 80–82°F., some of the cocoa butter solidifies into very fine crystals, too fine to see but making the couverture thicker. At this point, if you put a dab of couverture on a plate it would set almost immediately and commence to harden. The couverture would have to be stirred fairly continuously to keep it mixed and in a fluid state and it would be too thick to use for coating chocolates. It has to be warmed gently and slowly, stirring constantly until sufficient of the cocoa butter has melted again to thin the couverture. The temperature will now be above 85°F. However, if the temperature of the couverture is allowed to exceed 91°F. there is every likelihood that too much cocoa butter will melt, it will take too long to set and the cocoa particles will tend to sink and the surface will become mottled with the pure cocoa butter rising to the top.

The dairy butter which is added to milk couverture does not affect the problems of tempering except that it makes the couverture softer, dairy butter having a lower melting point than cocoa butter; therefore the final working temperature must be lower, below 88°F., or the couverture will be too thin.

Should the temperature of plain couverture accidentally exceed 91°F. (88°F. for milk couverture) while it is being used, it will be noticeable that it quickly runs off the centre that is being coated and takes much longer to set. The only solution is to cool the chocolate again to 80–82°F. and warm it once more to the working temperature. These maximum working temperatures are therefore absolutely critical, and a great deal of time can be wasted warming and cooling couverture which has thinned because it accidentally became too hot.

The best temperature at which to use plain couverture seems to be between 88 and 90°F., and for milk couverture between 85 and 87°F. It is within these ranges that they are thick enough to set quickly, and thin enough to put an adequate but not excessive coating on chocolate centres.

PRACTICAL CHOCOLATE TEMPERING

The equipment required includes:

1. A double-boiler or a similar arrangement such that one basin or pan fits on top of the other and the base can hold at least inch of water without the upper part coming into contact with the water. I was fortunate enough to find some cheap casserole dishes made of aluminium which sit about $\frac{3}{4}$ in. inside each other and are admirable for the purpose.
2. A plain glass thermometer, not a sugar-boiling thermometer. Boots sell one by Brannan which ranges from 0–240°F. Any glass thermometer with the range of from 80–125°F. would be suitable. However, the accuracy of thermometers can vary from day to day, so it is useful to have one which registers above the boiling-point of water (212°F. at sea level, 1°F. less for each increase of 550 feet in altitude) so that you can check it every time you use it. The best way to do this is to put it in at least 3 in. of cold water in a pan and bring it to the boil. Never put a cold thermometer into boiling water nor a hot one into cold water. Let the water boil fast for a few minutes then read off the temperature according to the thermometer. The thermometer should read 212°F. but if it reads, say, 210°F., you should add 2°F. to any other reading and use that as the actual temperature.
3. A board with a smooth, non-porous surface such as formica or marble, measuring 16 x 12 in. or more.
4. A flexible plastic spatula.

Put an inch or so of water into the base of the double-boiler. If it is made of aluminium, a pinch of powdered citric acid or a dash of vinegar or lemon juice will prevent staining. Place it over heat until bubbles start to rise to the surface – the temperature will be about 150–160°F. Turn the heat very low or remove it from the heat entirely.

Meanwhile, break up or chop at least 1 lb. of couverture into small pieces (you will need about ½ lb. to coat 1–1¼ lb. of centres), put the couverture in the top of the double-boiler and put this over the hot water. Make quite sure no steam or condensation gets into the couverture because the slightest drop will make it thicken and it will become useless for coating or 'dipping' chocolates. In fact, if you notice your couverture turning lighter in colour and thickening slightly it is almost certain that a minute quantity of water has got in from somewhere and you should make every effort to discover the source and stop it happening again.

The couverture will require stirring frequently to hasten melting and to ensure that no part gets overheated. In fact, couverture needs a lot of stirring at all stages especially while you are dipping, but always stir slowly so as not to get more air-bubbles into it than you can help. If you do get a lot, they are difficult to get out, but the best method seems to be to bang the bottom of the basin on something fairly solid, such as your knee, for a little time. This settles the couverture and forces the bubbles to the surface.

In cold weather, the water under the couverture will have to be reheated a time or two. When it is fully melted, check with the thermometer, ensuring it is quite dry before putting it in. Keep warming and stirring the couverture until the temperature is about 115°F., remembering that it must never exceed 120°F.

Now take the top from the double-boiler and carefully wipe underneath to remove all condensation. Pour at least two-thirds of the couverture in a pool on the formica board, which has been carefully cleaned and dried. Put the remaining couverture on one side in a cool, but not a cold place. Work the couverture about on the board with the plastic spatula until it cools and thickens, but try not to let any of it harden. Scrape the thickened couverture back into the top of the double-boiler and stir it in with the rest of the couverture until it is all quite smooth. Take the temperature with the thermometer. It must not be more than 90°F.; if it is, you will have to pour it out on the board to cool again. If the temperature is below 86°F., the couverture will be too thick to use and it will have to be warmed slightly. This is where most care needs to be exercised. Bring the water in the double-boiler to 94 or 95°F., remove from the heat, and put the couverture over it. Keep stirring slowly until the couverture temperature rises to 88–90°. At this point, the couverture should be properly tempered and ready for use.

To summarise briefly: first, melt the couverture to 115–120°F., then cool it to 80–82°F. and finally warm it to 88–90°F. Perhaps the following chart will help to make it clear.

Chocolate Temperature Chart

°F.

120	Maximum temperature
115	Chocolate fully melted
93	Too thin to use
90	Maximum working temperature for plain couverture
88	Maximum working temperature for milk couverture
85	Minimum working temperature for plain couverture
83	Minimum working temperature for milk couverture
82 }⟩	Couverture sets and begins to harden
80	
65	Normal room temperature

Professional chocolatiers can tell by the look of the couverture whether it is tempered. The infallible check is to dip some centres; by the time the fifth or sixth is coated, the first should have dimmed over and begun to set. However, if you put a dab of couverture on a sheet of wax or silicone paper with the end of your thermometer, it should go slightly dim in less than 90 seconds. If it dims more quickly, the couverture is too thick and should be warmed very carefully. If it takes a little longer and

33

you detect a slight streak, it is slightly too warm and in danger of thinning. A tip given to me by a professional chocolatier is very useful in this case; drop in a couple of lumps of broken couverture about the size of chestnuts and stir for a few moments. If it takes much more than 100 seconds to set, the couverture is not tempered and will discolour.

As you become more experienced in tempering couverture you will find it unnecessary to use the thermometer, except for melting the couverture initially to 115–120°F. You will also find it easier to cool the couverture by putting the pan in cold water for a few moments at a time and stirring, being careful not to let it lump. A dab of couverture on your bottom lip will tell you when it is cool enough. You will also find it quicker to warm the couverture to a working temperature by putting the pan over direct heat for a brief time. There are short-cuts, but only for the experienced. I once put some couverture to melt in a slow oven to save time. Condensation formed inside the oven and in the couverture, making it useless for dipping.

Once a quantity of couverture has been tempered, more un-tempered couverture can be added, provided this has been melted to 115–120°F. and then cooled to not more than 90°F. (88°F. for milk couverture). In this condition, up to 10 lb. of untempered couverture can be added to 1 lb. of tempered, or you can add small quantities frequently, since the tempered couverture will temper the freshly melted couverture. If you have any left over at the end of dipping, it can always be poured out to set on wax or silicone paper and then remelted when you wish to use it again.

CHOCOLATE DIPPING

Having prepared the couverture, it is important to keep it at the right temperature. Thermostatically-controlled pans are available but expensive, and it is quite effective to keep the couverture in the top of the double-boiler and maintain the water in the base at 94°F. or so, adding hot or cold water when necessary. If you have a food warmer, the double-boiler could be kept on that.

Since it is essential to prevent moisture getting into the couverture, it is not a good plan to dip centres when the atmosphere is damp since tiny quantities get in and affect the gloss. Make sure, therefore, that as much steam as possible is excluded from the room in which you are working and try not to dip when the weather is wet or muggy. However, at least the couverture will set in these conditions even if it becomes dull and slightly grey – and probably only another chocolatier would notice this. But if the temperature of the room is too high it is very serious, for in this case the couverture will take too long to set and will turn really grey.

The best room temperature is from 65 to 67°F., and you can obtain that temperature at most times of the year by the use of heaters in winter or opening windows in summer. You will quickly become quite practised at gauging the temperature and soon aware of slight temperature changes, but you will need to keep an eye on a thermometer at first. If the room temperature exceeds 70°F. you will begin to have serious setting problems, and it would be wise to move any centres you have dipped into a cold place (but not the 'fridge) until you have got the room temperature under control again. Some authorities claim the finest gloss is obtained when the difference between the temperature of the room and the temperature of the couverture is exactly 22°F. In other words, if the tempered couverture is 89°F., the room temperature should be 67°F.

Lastly, the temperature of the centres you are going to dip is important. If they are too warm, they transmit heat to the couverture and delay setting. If they are too cold, the couverture sets too quickly and loses its gloss. In addition, you will have trouble with the centre being compressed by the contracting coating of couverture as described for Truffles on p. 22, and either the couverture will crack or, if it is a soft centre, it will squeeze out through some weak spot.

Fortunately, the temperature of the centres is not as critical as the temperatures of the room and the couverture, and if the centres are brought into the dipping-room an hour or two before-hand there should be no problem. Also, it helps if you hold the centre a moment or two to warm in your hand before dropping it into the couverture.

As I have emphasised, the problem of the temperature of the couverture and the factors which can affect it are extremely important. It is infuriating to find, too late, that something has gone wrong. I remember filling a tray with chocolates, newly dipped, a few inches away from a hot coffee percolator. There was just enough heat from the percolator to delay some of the chocolate setting. It was some time later, after I had moved the tray to another room, that I noticed all the chocolates within a radius of about 6 in. had set grey and cloudy. Of course, it is possible to dip them again, but this does make an excessively thick coating.

At this stage it would be advisable to practise dipping, using some simple centres. Perhaps the easiest are nuts – brazil nuts and half walnuts are ideal. Or some pieces of preserved ginger could be removed from the syrup, cut into convenient pieces and dried carefully. Alternatively, it would not be cheating to buy a quarter of nougat or caramels from a sweet shop and use them. Make sure, with any centre, there is no loose material which could become mixed in with the couverture and spoil it.

You will also need some wax paper or silicone paper to put your centres on after they have been dipped. Greaseproof will not do, since the chocolate adheres. Wax paper is widely available in rolls from stationers who stock wrapping-paper, shelf-paper and the like. Some, made in Denmark under the name 'Colorit', is washable and heavy enough for our purpose; it is available, too, in white. Silicone paper can also be obtained from stationers, usually in a packet containing several sheets. 'Bakewell Household Vegetable Parchment' is one brand. Silicone paper does not stand up to wetting as well as wax paper and is expensive, but it is more useful since it does not stick to anything with a high sugar content such as toffees.

36

If you are right-handed, it is helpful to put the centres on your left and a sheet of wax or silicone paper on a board on your right and keep your tempered chocolate in front of you. Having checked all your temperatures – the room, the couverture and the water under it as well as the centres – you are ready to start dipping.

I prefer to 'pre-bottom' all centres. This is, smear a thin coating of couverture over what will be the bottom of the centre with the back of a spoon, and place it, bottom-side up, on another plate or board. Then dip it fully in couverture later. There are three reasons for this. Firstly, it makes quite sure that the couverture is properly tempered, because after pre-bottoming the fifth or sixth, the first should be beginning to set. If it is not, nothing is wasted except time, since the couverture can be retempered before the centre is fully dipped. Secondly, when chocolates are deposited on the wax sheets, one corner may sink slightly more than the rest of the base and set with only a very thin skin of chocolate, which can easily break, permitting the centre to leak. Thirdly, pre-bottoming gives a firm base for dipping soft centres which might otherwise be difficult to lift out of the couverture pan.

After the bases have set and hardened a little, stir the couverture thoroughly, trying not to get too many air-bubbles in. Drop a centre into the couverture, bottom down and with an ordinary household fork, slightly warmed, push it down to submerge it thoroughly. Immediately, pick it out with the fork, keeping it the right way up and bringing it as near to the point of the prongs as possible without its falling off. Tap the fork on the side of the basin or on the spoon in order to settle the couverture, and wipe any excess from underneath the fork. Transfer the centre to the wax or silicone sheet. Put the tip of the prongs down on the sheet and gradually ease the fork away, giving the centre a little push forward to level it out. Stir the couverture after depositing each centre to keep it well mixed.

If the couverture looks very glossy and starts to run off the centre to form a pool on the sheet, it has thinned out and will have to be retempered. The fork should be kept warm because it may otherwise chill the couverture, making the centre stick to the fork and impossible to deposit. If the fork is too hot, it can melt the base and sink into a soft centre.

After all the centres have been dipped, it is an advantage to move them to another cool room to harden. The temperature must not be more than 65°F. but can be very much lower. However, the refrigerator is too cold and can result in 'sugar bloom'. This is caused when chocolates are moved from a cold atmosphere to a warm one which has a higher level of humidity. Condensation forms on the cold chocolates and dissolves minute particles of sugar. When the moisture evaporates again, the sugar is deposited as a fine powder over the surface of the chocolate and discolours it. Chocolates subjected to heat, such as from direct sunlight, suffer from 'fat bloom' when the cocoa butter on the surface melts and allows the cocoa particles to sink. This appears as a greyish-white discoloration, occasionally seen in sweetshop windows. None of these mishaps affects in any way the edibility or even the flavour of the chocolate, but any kind of food seems to taste better if it looks attractive. 'We eat with our eyes', a chef once told me.

A household fork is adequate for first efforts at dipping, but you will need a set of four, or possibly more, different kinds of the special dipping forks. They are not easy to find but they are stocked by:

Messrs Creeds (Southern) Ltd., Pulteney Road, South Woodford, London E.18 (Tel. 01–530 2191) and

Messrs Creeds (Northern) Ltd., 1 Stanley Road, Birkenhead, Cheshire (Tel. 051–652 6068).

The most useful are the two-, three- and four-pronged forks and a ring-fork.

Dipping-forks can be made fairly easily if you can use a soldering iron. You will need a 7-in. length of copper tube for each handle, which can be obtained from an ironmonger or builders' suppliers. There are two useful sizes, $\frac{3}{16}$ in. diameter

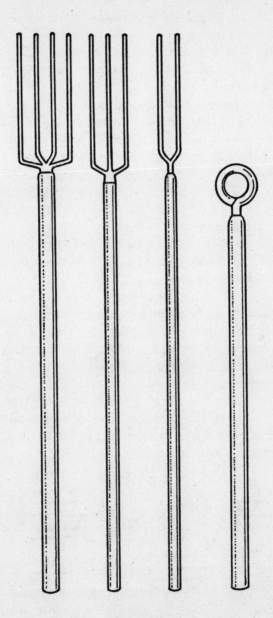

Dipping Forks

with a 3/32 in. bore, and a $\frac{1}{4}$ in. diameter with a bore of 5/32 in. This latter is supplied in a roll-like cable, but is not difficult to straighten. You will also need two or three lengths of $\frac{1}{16}$ in. welding wire for the prongs, from a motor repair garage or a blacksmith. Also, a screw-eye for the ring-fork, preferably chromed to prevent rust; a good size of ring has an overall diameter of $\frac{5}{8}$ in. and the hole a diameter of $\frac{3}{8}$ in. Take a piece of the thicker copper tube and make four saw cuts along the length of the tube from one end for about $\frac{3}{4}$ in. Put the screw of the screw-eye inside the tube at the cut end and press the flaps over it. The saw cuts are necessary because the diameter of the bore is greater than that of the screw-eye. Then solder the flaps to the screw-eye.

The prongs of the forks have to be fashioned from the welding wire. For the double-pronged fork, take a length about 7 in. long and bend it in two. About $\frac{3}{4}$ in. from the bend, part the two prongs to form the shoulders, then bend again to form the tines which should be about $\frac{1}{4}$ in. apart when finished and about $2\frac{1}{8}$ in long. File down the wire for $\frac{1}{2}$ in. from the bend until it is thin enough to penetrate a length of the $\frac{3}{16}$-in. diameter copper tube, then solder it in and smooth down.

The principle of making the three- and four-pronged forks is the same, but the end of a length of $\frac{3}{16}$-in. tube should be flattened to make the bore oval, so that it will take the three prongs more easily. The four-pronged fork is fitted into the $\frac{1}{4}$-in. diameter tube. The wires are bent as follows:

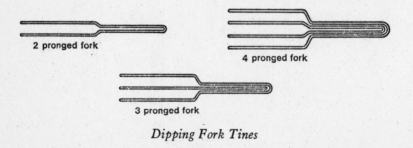

2 pronged fork

4 pronged fork

3 pronged fork

Dipping Fork Tines

Again, the tines are about $2\frac{1}{8}$ in. long and up to $\frac{1}{4}$ in. apart. To finish, the copper handle can be cleaned with some copper polish and then given a thin coat of cellulose varnish or clear nail varnish which should also cover the solder.

HOW TO USE DIPPING FORKS

The dipping fork is not only used for lifting the centre out of the bowl of couverture but is also the means by which the tops of chocolates are decorated after they have been deposited on the wax or silicone sheet.

The pronged forks are easy to use. After submerging the centre in the couverture, pick it out with the two-, three- or four-pronged fork, depending on how many lines you want the chocolate to have. Then transfer it to the sheet and deposit it as previously described, easing the fork gently away from under the centre. Finally, lay the prongs just to touch the surface of the chocolate, lift slightly and draw the fork away in the direction you wish the lines to follow. For a single line, just use one prong of whichever fork is most convenient to lift the centre out of the couverture.

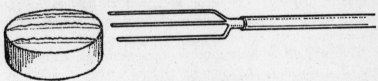

Marking Chocolates

Another and quicker way to use the fork is to invert the chocolate quickly over the sheet so that the prongs are on top of the centre. The marks of the prongs are made automatically as the fork is taken away. If you intend to work this way, pre-bottomed centres have to be dropped into the couverture bottom-side up.

The ring-fork is used to put the twirly shapes or 'thread' on the chocolate and is much more difficult to handle correctly.

The centre is dropped in the couverture in the usual way, submerged and picked out with the ring-fork and transferred to the sheet. Here, it is always inverted and allowed to drop on to the sheet with the ring on top. As you remove the ring, you collect the excess couverture in a blob on the surface of the chocolate, lift slightly, and make a little trail. If there is not enough couverture, pick up a little more from the pan with the ring-fork. These centres should be 'pre-topped' rather than 'pre-bottomed' since there is little risk of the centre coming through the base of the chocolate, but it is quite easy for the ring to scrape off too much couverture from the top of the centre and if the top has been coated beforehand there is no risk of leaks. With a little practice you will be able to make a letter 'C', and later the more complicated 'R' for raspberry, 'L' for lemon or lime, 'S' for strawberry and so on. But do not be disappointed at your first efforts, these are imperfections which only another chocolatier would notice.

HAND-DIPPING

Some professional chocolatiers do not use forks but dip by hand rather as the truffles were coated in Chapter 1. This method has some advantages – fewer problems with air-bubbles, for instance, and it is perhaps easier to deal with soft centres, but it is sometimes regarded as messy and unhygienic.

The method is to have a supply of couverture melted to 115–120°F. and then cooled to 90–92°F. Pour a small quantity, say ¼ lb. or thereabouts, on to a formica or marble slab and work it about until it thickens. Add some more melted couverture and mix well with the fingers of the right hand (if right-handed). This will temper it, and adding the warmer couverture will thin it out sufficiently. Drop a centre on the fingers of your right hand and coat it thoroughly, picking up more couverture from the slab if necessary. Then the centre can be pushed to the tips of the fingers and the knuckles knocked on the slab to settle the couverture before transferring it to the depositing sheet. The centre can be put down, with the hand still palm upwards, by pushing it off the tips of the fingers with the thumb. Alternatively, the centre can be transferred to the sheet, the hand turned palm down and the centre allowed to drop. The thread can be made with the thumb, by picking up a blob from the surface of the centre and trailing it in the desired shape. The centre should be deposited quickly or the warmth of the fingers can thin the couverture too much and it sets with streaks. As the couverture on the slab cools and thickens, more warm couverture is added to thin it and is thoroughly mixed in, tempering it as it is being incorporated.

A packet of mixed dried fruit from the grocer's can be dipped in this way, or sultanas and currants and a few chopped nuts. Take a few pieces and moisten them with couverture, then drop them in rough shapes on the depositing sheet.

With this method, it is just as important to keep the room temperature constant at 65–67°F.

Having learned how to use couverture for chocolates, you may wish to employ your skill in other ways. Biscuits can be bought or made at home and dipped in couverture, which can also be used to decorate small cakes, but it must be remembered that couverture sets hard and cannot be cut, so that for larger cakes baking chocolate is more suitable. Also, be careful not to allow loose crumbs to get into the couverture.

Another way in which couverture can be used is for casting in moulds of various shapes, and once you know how to temper it, the principles of using chocolate in this way become quite simple, whether you are making large Easter eggs or small bottle-shaped liqueurs.

EASTER-EGGS AND OTHER MOULDS

Moulds used to be made of metal, but plastic is cheaper, easier to use and maintain and gives a better finish. Creeds (see p. 149) also supply a range of moulds in a variety of sizes. Occasionally it is possible to obtain them from other sources, and the manufacturers of 'Cakebrand' baking chocolate offer a small selection to purchasers of their product. Any glossy, plastic, concave shape

43

can be used as a mould. This material is sometimes used as packing for various products such as cosmetics, and occasionally this packing is made in shapes which are suitable for chocolate moulds.

Small moulds are usually filled with tempered couverture and then inverted and allowed to drain. If using a larger mould, it is more convenient to pour into it just sufficient couverture to coat it, and then pick up the mould and move it around so that the pool of couverture covers the whole inside. It is then inverted over silicone or wax paper, not so much in order to allow it to drain as to encourage a thick rim at the edge which is very useful when putting the two halves of an egg or other kind of mould together. The mould should be tapped to try to encourage air-bubbles to rise, and where this is very important – for chocolate liqueurs, for instance – a skin of couverture can be brushed on the inside of the moulds beforehand.

The chocolate shell must be allowed to harden thoroughly before attempting to remove it from the mould. As couverture hardens, it also contracts and pulls away from the mould sufficiently to loosen it. If, therefore, the chocolate shell cannot be made to drop away from the mould easily, it is very likely that it has not completely set and must be left a little longer. Under no circumstances should you attempt to scratch the chocolate away from the mould, since this will damage the surface of the mould. The high gloss achieved on chocolate by the use of moulds depends entirely on their glossy surface, and if this is damaged the chocolate shells will be affected. Moulds can, of course, be washed in detergent and dried after being rinsed in clean water.

3

Sugar-Boiling

Most chocolate centres are made from sugar and water. Various other ingredients are added for flavour and texture but the basis is sugar and water, and in order to make centres successfully it is necessary to understand how sugar and water behave in various circumstances. For instance, fudge and caramels are made from very similar materials; the difference is that fudge has a crystalline texture, therefore it is necessary to know how to create that texture when making fudge, and, equally important, how to avoid it when making caramels.

Approximately 15 oz. of granulated sugar can be dissolved in $\frac{1}{2}$ pint of cold water. In other words, cold water will hold one and a half times its own weight of sugar in solution. Hot water, however, can hold a much greater quantity of sugar, and $\frac{1}{2}$ pint of boiling water can dissolve as much as $2\frac{1}{2}$ lb. of granulated sugar or four times its own weight. At this point no more sugar can be dissolved and it is known as a 'super-saturated' solution. If more sugar were to be added, it would just remain in crystal form in the solution no matter how much stirring you did and even though you increased the temperature substantially. So the warmer the solution, the more sugar can be dissolved in it, up to a point. Beyond that point, no more sugar will dissolve. Conversely, a super-saturated solution of sugar which is then cooled can no longer hold all its sugar, which then begins to fall out of solution into crystals resembling dry sugar again. This

45

does not necessarily happen immediately, it may take some little time, but it is bound to happen eventually.

This tendency of sugar solutions to crystallise, or 'grain' as it is called, is of great importance in sugar confectionery. Professional sugar boilers know exactly how graining can be controlled, and how it can be encouraged to produce different kinds of sweets.

The most usual way of controlling grain is by adding what is called a 'doctor' to the sugar solution. There is a large range of doctors which are used in various strengths depending upon the desired result. Some have other useful characteristics, such as reducing the sweetness of the solution to make it less sickly. There are broadly two types of doctor, sugar substances which do not crystallise readily and acids or acid substances.

The acids are normally food acids, such as acetic acid found naturally in vinegar, citric acid from citrus fruits such as lemons, or tartaric acid from grapes. Cream of tartar, an acid substance, is also often used. All these must be added in very small quantities because they are very drastic, but in hard-water areas slightly larger quantities have to be used since some of the acid is neutralised by the alkalinity of the water. Acetic acid has a pungent smell, which is a further reason for it to be used only in weak solutions. Commercially, acids are not preferred because they are erratic and do not always produce consistent results, but in small quantities, for home cooking, they are less unsatisfactory: $\frac{1}{8}$ to $\frac{3}{16}$ of a teaspoonful of cream of tartar is adequate for 1 lb. sugar. Acids work by chemically changing some of the sugar into non-crystallisable sugar known as 'invert sugar', and should make enough invert sugar to prevent the rest crystallising too quickly.

The most widely used doctor is one of the sugar substances, known as confectioner's glucose, liquid glucose or corn syrup, and is a clear liquid so thick that the surface almost feels dry to the touch. It is normally produced from cornflour – although potato starch can be used – by a chemical process involving the use of acid. Being considerably less sweet than granulated sugar, it helps to make sweets less sickly and is added in fairly large amounts, usually 1 part of glucose to 4 parts of sugar, though the proportions can be varied considerably and without ill effects. Where a production method involves a high risk of graining, a proportion of 1 part of glucose to 1 part of sugar can be used. Liquid glucose is also hygroscopic; it tends to absorb moisture from the atmosphere. This is an advantage in fudges and fondants since it helps to keep them moist, but it means that hard toffees such as butterscotch must be kept wrapped or coated or they become sticky. Glucose also helps to make sweets more chewy and longer-lasting.

Other sugar substances can be employed because they do not crystallise readily and inhibit sugar from crystallising. Glycerine is used but rarely. Invert sugar can be included in much the same quantities as liquid glucose. Invert sugar is manufactured commercially by the process mentioned earlier, of boiling an acid with sugar, but under controlled conditions the amount of inversion is more consistent and the effects more predictable. Brown sugar contains some invert sugar, which is why it behaves as though it is slightly damp; so do golden syrup, treacle and molasses, but these are not used as doctors since the amounts of invert sugar in them are variable and their effects are not consistent. They are, however, good for flavouring. Honey is a natural form of invert sugar and can be used as a doctor, but it is very expensive and, again, is normally included only for flavouring.

The home sweetmaker will probably find liquid glucose very difficult to obtain since it is normally supplied only to the trade. Boots sell it as 'Liquid Glucose BP' in 1-lb. jars, but it is very expensive and may have to be ordered specially. The doctor most easily available outside the trade, and which has all the advantages of liquid glucose, is available in powder form as 'Glucose'. Its chemical name is Dextrose Monohydrate and it is manufactured from the same materials as liquid glucose but by an extended and slightly different process. The fact that it is obtained as a powder indicates that it can be made to crystallise, but the point is that it does not crystallise easily, and when dissolved in water and added to a sugar syrup it effectively inhibits the sugar from crystallising in just the same way as liquid glucose. When used for making fondant, glucose gives a softer and whiter result than liquid glucose, but it has to be used in smaller quantities, 1 part of glucose to 5 or 6 parts of sugar is normally adequate.

A form of liquid glucose can be purchased from a few shops under the name 'Crown Brand Corn Syrup', in 1-lb. and 2-lb. jars. This is a thinner syrup than the commercial variety, containing 74 per cent as compared with 80 per cent sugar solids. It has an amber colour but is quite suitable for use as a doctor instead of liquid glucose where colour does not matter – you could not use it for making clear mints or fondant, for instance, but it is quite all right for caramels or fudges. It is not easy to obtain, but I have bought it from Selfridge's and Fortnum and Mason's and from Hannell's Stores, Davies Street, London W.1.

It is also necessary to know how to *encourage* grain, particularly for making fudge and fondant. A smaller proportion of the doctor is used, but a certain amount is essential or the result will be very coarse crystals instead of a soft, smooth texture. There are two methods of causing grain, known as 'agitation' and 'seeding'. With both methods, the sugar syrup to which the doctor has been added is brought to a predetermined temperature and is then allowed to cool.

With the agitation method, the syrup is then stirred or folded over itself until it begins to cloud a little. As the stirring continues, the syrup thickens and becomes a hard, opaque mass.

The seeding method consists of adding a crystalline substance such as fondant or icing sugar to the slightly cooled syrup – the amount is not critical – and stirring it in. The syrup will thicken and become opaque quite quickly; moreover, the crystals of the finished product will resemble those which were added, so that, if icing sugar were added, the result would be a fine-grained fudge, but if granulated sugar were added, it would be very coarse. It will be seen, therefore, that when trying to avoid grain it is necessary to stir the syrup as little as possible, if at all, and to be very careful not to permit any stray sugar crystals to get into the syrup after it has begun to boil.

SUGAR TEMPERATURES

The degree of hardness of toffees and caramels depends entirely on their water content. A soft caramel or fudge contains more water than a hard toffee such as treacle toffee, which is itself softer and contains more water than butterscotch. It is important to know how to control and also how to measure the water content of a syrup.

A hydrometer can be used to measure precisely what the strength of a sugar and water syrup may be, but it takes time to obtain a reading. A refractometer, which can measure the proportion of solids in any liquid, is simple to use, extremely accurate and has every advantage except it is very expensive. For most sugar work, a sugar thermometer is accurate enough when properly used, gives an instant reading and is easily obtainable and not too expensive.

Starting from a cold sugar syrup which, as we have seen, will contain about 15 oz. of sugar to $\frac{1}{2}$ pint of water, if heat is applied it will eventually reach a fast boil. On an accurate thermometer, at sea-level, the temperature will be 215°F. or more. Pure water boils at the slightly lower temperature of 212°F. If the syrup is kept boiling, the water will evaporate into steam and the syrup will become more highly concentrated. At the same time the temperature of the solution will increase; in fact, there is a direct relationship under these circumstances between the amount of water left and the temperature. Indeed, if the temperature of a boiling syrup read 250°F. and a teaspoonful of boiling water were added, the temperature would fall, and would only return to 250°F. when a teaspoonful of water, precisely, had evaporated.

It is possible to draw up a table which compares the hardness of various sweets with their final cooking temperatures.

Temperature
Degree Fahrenheit

Caramel	310	Sugar begins to brown
	305	
Hard Crack	300 ⎫ 295 ⎬ 290 ⎪ 285 ⎭	Confection is very brittle and crunchy e.g. butterscotch, barley sugar
Soft Crack	280 ⎫ 275 ⎬ 270 ⎭	Sweets are very hard and chewy e.g. hard caramels, treacle toffee
	265	
Hard Ball	260	Medium-hard caramels
	255	
	250	
Soft ball	245 ⎫ 240 ⎭	Soft caramels, candy Fondant, fudge
	235	
	230	
Sugar syrup boils depending on concentration	225 ⎫ 220 ⎬ 215 ⎭	
Water boils	212	

Hardness can be tested by dropping a small quantity of syrup into very cold water and allowing it to chill. Professionals can pick out a blob of boiling syrup with their fingers and plunge it into cold water, but that is very risky for the inexperienced. The 'Degrees' listed in the table are some of the standard terms used to describe the consistency of a small sample of syrup cooked to the corresponding temperature and chilled.

If a syrup should accidentally reach a temperature higher

than you intended, you can always add a little boiling water (cold water would make it explode), and continue cooking until you reach the correct temperature again. Any sweet can be recooked in this way except nougats or marshmallows after albumen has been added, because the albumen burns at relatively low temperatures.

The principle of sugar-boiling illustrated in the table is important in another way. If a flavour is added to a boiling syrup, being liquid it tends to thin it, and if you continue boiling to get the syrup back to the original degree, the flavour usually boils away and is lost. In fact, there are specially manufactured flavours which withstand high temperatures, but they are available only in the trade. One of the methods of solving this problem is to cook the syrup beyond the final temperature, so that it is thicker than necessary, then cool it until the flavour can be safely added, thus thinning the syrup to the correct consistency.

A syrup made from 1 lb. of granulated sugar dissolved in water and cooked to 240°F. will weigh approximately 1 lb. $2\frac{1}{2}$ oz. In other words, there is 1 lb. of sugar and $2\frac{1}{2}$ oz. of water. If the syrup is cooked further, the water will gradually boil away, giving the following approximate weights of syrup at each temperature:

240°	1 lb. $2\frac{1}{2}$ oz.
245°	1 lb. 2 oz.
250°	1 lb. $1\frac{3}{4}$ oz.
260°	1 lb. $1\frac{3}{8}$ oz.
270°	1 lb. 1 oz.
285°	1 lb. $0\frac{5}{8}$ oz.
300°	1 lb. $0\frac{1}{2}$ oz.

When cooked to 270°F., which is 'soft crack' degree the water content would be only 1 oz. If a further 1 oz. of water were added, the syrup would thin to what it had been at 245°F., which is soft ball. Therefore, if a syrup were cooked to 270°F., it could be cooled and 1 oz. of water, or 1 oz. of a flavour with a similar consistency to water, could be stirred in. The total quantity of liquid would be 2 oz. and the result would be a syrup thick enough to make fudge or candy or a very soft caramel. Looking at it another way, if you are planning to make a candy using 1 lb. granulated sugar or 1 lb. sugar and glucose mixed (the glucose makes no difference to this principle), and in order to give a good flavour you need to add 1 oz. of some flavouring liquid which is about as thin as water, you will have to cook the syrup to 270°F. before cooling it to add the flavour. The consistency will be the same as if you had only cooked the syrup to 245°F. in the first place and added no flavour.

If the flavouring agent is a fruit concentrate or purée it will be much thicker than water and you could add more than 1 oz. On the other hand, some liquids, such as spirits, are thinner than water and adding 1 oz. would thin the syrup too much. There are limits to this sort of exercise. Suppose you wanted a caramel which sets as hard as if you cooked it to 270°F. but you wanted to add 1 oz. of flavouring liquid as thin as water. It would mean boiling the syrup above 300°F. to evaporate all the water, so that when adding the 1 oz. of flavour the total weight would return to 1 lb. 1 oz. In fact, if the syrup were heated above 300°F. it would begin to burn, so that in practice you would either have to settle for a softer caramel or put less flavour in.

These figures are fairly approximate, but they give an indication of the effect of adding a liquid to a syrup and illustrate the very important fact that flavours need to be as concentrated as possible otherwise they thin the mixture too much.

SUGAR-BOILING EQUIPMENT

For any kind of sugar confectionery the following equipment is essential. The first four items will be stocked by any kitchen equipment store.

1. A sugar-boiling thermometer. The thermometer recommended for tempering chocolate will not do. This thermo-

meter must be mounted on a metal frame on which is printed the degrees of temperature, each mark usually indicating 5 degrees. It must range from 100–325°F., and most sugar thermometers range well over 400°F. although at this temperature sugar would be a smoky black mass. Brannan make a 'Universal Cookmeter' which, instead of having the usual metal cage over the bulb, has a metal plate which can easily be removed. This is an advantage, since syrup sometimes thickens inside the cage and insulates the bulb, giving an inaccurate reading.

2. A set of scales. There is a variety of makes and types. It should weigh up to 3 lb. at least and be graduated in $\frac{1}{4}$-oz. sections. I find the best scales are those with an arm across the front which have two sliding weights to indicate ounces and pounds. There is usually a weighted rod at the side which can be pulled out of the body of the scales to counterbalance any container. You can put any size of pan or bowl on the scales, counterbalance it so that it weighs nil, and then weigh off the ingredients into the bowl in the usual way. This is a very valuable piece of equipment.

3. Saucepans. You probably have a stock of these anyway. The most useful are the ones with a lip round the edge since they do not drip. A 6-in. pan, which will hold about 3 pints and a 5-in. pan, which will hold just under 2 pints, are necessary. The 5-in. should be about $3\frac{1}{2}$ in. deep; it is really for the thermometer – a shallower pan might allow the thermometer to topple out. A 7-in pan, holding about $4\frac{1}{2}$ pints, is useful for large quantities or for caramels and fudges which tend to boil over.

4. Pastry-brush. Preferably the wooden-handled variety. They are quite cheap and a couple would come in handy for washing down the sides of the pan to ensure that all the sugar is dissolved, and for washing syrup off the thermometer.

5. It is essential to have something to pour the hot syrup on to permit it to set. The temperature of the syrup can be anything from 240 to 310°F. and it must be chilled as soon

as it comes into contact with the surface it is being poured on to. If the syrup is allowed to heat this surface too much it will adhere, and when it sets it will have to be chipped off. A sheet of formica on plywood will serve for temperatures up to about 250°F. Alternatively, a rectangular metal container can be used set in cold water, but the water will have to be changed as it absorbs heat from the syrup. The best surface is one which does not absorb heat very easily, such as marble or slate. New marble is very expensive but it may still be possible to pick up an old marble-topped wash-stand for a pound or two from a junk dealer. The marble should be $\frac{3}{4}$ in. thick or more and should be at least 18 in. square, although it could be narrower provided it was longer. Marble is extremely heavy, not to be carried long distances. If you only want the top of a wash-stand, the dealer will probably unscrew it for you and dispose of the rest, but if it has a good-sized drawer, say 16 x 16 in., keep it for a 'starch tray' for casting the fondants we will be discussing later on.

6. You will also need four straight iron bars. Ideally, they should be $\frac{3}{4}$ in. square but can be 1 in. square, and 12–15 in. long; 15 in. is particularly convenient. They can be bought from a blacksmith cut to the length you want. They will probably be very dirty with rust and it would be wise to ask the blacksmith to clean them. Sandpaper or emery-cloth is hopeless, it requires a wire wheel attachment to an electric drill, out of doors, but not when there is washing out to dry.

The bars can be greased and arranged on the marble or formica to give any size of rectangle, as shown in the diagram.

The syrup is then poured between the bars, which can be adjusted to give the required depth of syrup. When it sets, all the corners are nicely squared off and there are no odd shapes. The disadvantage of using metal tins is that you either have too much syrup for the depth you want, or too little, and there is waste at the corners, but, of course, when using metal tins it is not necessary to have the bars.

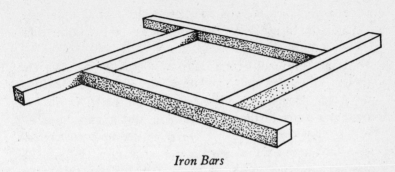

Iron Bars

PRACTICAL SUGAR-BOILING

Boiling sugar is not difficult, but there are pitfalls. This step-by-step procedure is designed to avoid them, and after you have done it the right way once or twice it will become automatic. Certainly, the right way is the easiest.

1. Assemble the equipment. Put the thermometer in the 5-in. pan, half-fill with cold water and bring to the boil. Have the pastry-brush and the pan to hold the syrup handy. Decide where you are to put the syrup when it is cooked, whether in a tin or on a formica or marble slab. Grease the surface and the iron bars with a light coating of vegetable oil or fat – but not butter.

2. Assemble the ingredients and weigh out the sugar, the doctoring agent and any necessary flavours. If you are making a caramel, you will need butter or evaporated or condensed milk.

3. The sugar can be weighed directly into the pan if your scales will allow this, together with the powdered glucose if that is the doctoring agent you are using. To this add an amount of water equal to one-quarter the weight of the sugar and glucose. If using 16 oz. of sugar and glucose together, you will need 4 oz. of water. One pint of water weighs 20 oz., so 4 oz. is just under ¼ pint. You can use more

55

water if you wish but you will have to boil the syrup longer. Do not try to use less or the sugar will not dissolve completely.

4. Heat the sugar and water, stirring constantly with a metal spoon – a wooden one may discolour the syrup – until all the sugar crystals are dissolved. Dip the pastry-brush into the clean water in the other pan and wash round the inside of the syrup pan to make sure there are no stray crystals about. You can tell if the sugar has dissolved by pressing the back of the spoon on the bottom of the pan – there should be no grittiness. When you are sure that all the sugar has dissolved, you can turn up the heat and boil the syrup as fast as possible, but not so fast that it boils over. An extra precaution is to put the lid on the pan immediately it starts to boil and leave it on for a minute or so. The steam will then condense under the lid and down the inside of the pan ensuring that no sugar crystals remain undissolved.

5. The syrup must never be stirred after it boils, for this encourages graining. The water in the other pan should be boiling by now and the thermometer should read 212°F. – if it does not, the other readings will have to be adjusted; a reading of 210°F. means that 2°F. has to be added to other readings to obtain the correct temperature. Put the thermometer in the syrup and boil until the temperature shows 225°F. Gently move the thermometer round the pan to make sure it is giving an accurate reading.

225°F. is the temperature at which liquid glucose or acid is added, if these are the doctoring agents you are using. The acid, if in powder or crystal form, should have been dissolved already in as little water as possible. The acid or the liquid glucose is simply poured into the boiling syrup but without stirring it, the boiling will mix everything thoroughly, and stirring would encourage grain. The doctor can be added earlier only when cooking small quantities; even so, liquid glucose should not be added until after all the sugar has been dissolved since it makes it more difficult to dissolve the sugar, and adding acid earlier increases the amount of sugar inversion through the longer boiling.

6. Butter or milk is normally added to the syrup after it has reached 245–250°F. or, in the case of very hard toffees, an even higher temperature. The mixture has to be stirred fairly constantly and the heat lowered after any kind of milk solids have been added or they will burn: it must be stirred slowly to try to minimise the risk of graining and, of course, a higher proportion of the doctor has to be used, although the fat in butter and milk itself helps to restrain graining. The reason for adding milk solids late in the cooking process is to reduce the amount of stirring necessary, but a certain period of cooking is required to develop the flavour fully.

7. The syrup is cooked as rapidly as possible to the final temperature. The temperature increases very slowly at first, but more rapidly after 225°F. and quite fast after 250°F., so the thermometer must be watched carefully. It can be moved about very gently in the pan to ensure an accurate reading. When the syrup has reached the desired temperature, the pan is removed from the heat, the thermometer taken out and replaced in the small pan of boiling water, and the base of the pan can be dipped into cold water for a few moments to check the boiling and then rested on a cool heatproof surface. Flavours and colours are added at this point, but flavours are very volatile and if the syrup is too hot they will evaporate, while if it is too cold the amount of stirring necessary to incorporate them will increase the risk of graining.

8. Pour the mixture out over the prepared surface, trying not to pour any of the syrup over itself, which encourages grain. Do not scrape out the pan, or if you do, do not add the scrapings to the rest of the mix because these last scrapings have a strong tendency to grain and they will affect the rest of the confection.

9. After the toffee has set, but before it has hardened, use a knife to make impressions on the surface of the toffee in

bite-sized pieces, cutting about $\frac{1}{16}$ in. or $\frac{1}{8}$ in. deep. When the toffee hardens, it can be turned over and tapped with a hammer, when it will break along the impressions. Softer caramels can be cut with a sharp knife lightly greased, after they have hardened. Professionals use a caramel cutter, which is rather like a rolling-pin but with a number of variable blades which can be set at a given distance apart. However, it is not worth buying one of these for home use.

10. Caramels and toffees should either be dipped, wrapped or put in air-tight containers quite soon, since they quickly absorb moisture from the atmosphere and become sticky. With fudges and candies this tendency is not so obvious and is actually an advantage, since it keeps them moist.

4

Caramels

Caramels are a mixture of sugar, water and fat. Milk solids are normally added for flavour and other additions may include nuts, dried fruit and flavourings, but sugar, water and fat are the basic ingredients.

I propose to take one basic, and quite delicious, cream-flavour caramel recipe and then suggest variations on it, making it harder, giving it other flavours and changing the basic ingredients to give different characteristics.

From the principles outlined in the last chapter, we know that the inherent tendency of sugar to crystallise has to be checked by the addition of an acid or a non-crystallisable sugar substance. In this recipe we will use powdered glucose. Acid is rarely used with milk in any case, since the milk would curdle. For the fat, we will use lightly salted butter. Butter helps to give a creamy flavour and salt butter is stronger than unsalted, the salt itself not being noticeable. Fat also helps to prevent the caramel sticking to the teeth.

Milk solids are found in cream, evaporated milk, condensed milk, dried milk and, of course, in fresh milk. Dried milk has to be dissolved in water and has the same disadvantage as fresh in that it has to be cooked too long in order to evaporate the high water content. Evaporated milk has a fairly high water content but is often recommended. I find it has a greater tendency to curdle during cooking and must be added gradually and stirred constantly, thus increasing the risk of granulation. Cream is expensive but otherwise satisfactory. This recipe uses full cream condensed milk which contains very little water but about 40 per cent sugar, and this has to be taken into account when calculating the amount of glucose required. The large sized tin, which makes about $1\frac{5}{8}$ pint of sweetened milk, holds about $13\frac{1}{2}$ oz. of condensed milk. Butter and milk also have the property of emulsifying fat to make it combine with sugar and water without separating. If other, non-dairy fats are used, an emulsifying agent is required such as a quantity of gelatine equal to 1 per cent of the total quantity of the mixture.

Basic Caramel Recipe

Equipment: 6-in. pan, 5-in. pan, small saucepan, thermometer, scales, pastry-brush, marble slab and iron bars or square tin 8 x 8 in. set in cold water. Wooden spatula.

Ingredients: 8 oz. granulated sugar
4 oz. glucose powder
6 oz. full cream sweetened condensed milk
2 oz. butter
vanilla flavour.

Method: Follow the sugar-boiling procedure given on pp. 55–8. Put the thermometer in a 5-in. pan, add cold water and put it over heat. Grease the marble slab and bars or the tin.

Weigh the sugar and glucose powder into a 6-in. pan and add enough water to dissolve them before boiling-point is reached – 4 oz. or just under $\frac{1}{4}$ pint will be ample. Weigh the condensed milk and butter into a small saucepan and place it over a low heat for a short time, just enough to melt the butter and thin the milk so that they can be mixed, but not enough to burn the milk or make it turn lumpy, which it does very easily. A better way is to put the saucepan in another pan containing hot water.

Heat the sugar and glucose, stirring frequently with a metal spoon to ensure that all crystals are dissolved. Wash down the sides of the pan with clean water, using the pastry-brush, and as the syrup reaches boiling-point the lid can be put on the pan for a few minutes. When the water in the pan with the thermometer has been boiling for a minute or two, check the temperature reading; it should be 212°F. Put the thermometer in the syrup. Cook the syrup rapidly to 255°F., a degree or two either way does not matter. Move the thermometer about occasionally to ensure an accurate reading. Remove the pan from the heat, return the thermometer to the other pan and add the butter and condensed milk mixture slowly. Lower the heat and put the pan on again. Allow the mixture to come back to the boil, this will mix it without stirring, but make sure it does not boil over. From this point it is very easy to burn the mixture and stirring increases the risk of grain; therefore use a wooden spatula with a straight edge on the bottom so that you can constantly scrape the base of the pan to prevent sticking and burning, but do it slowly so that you are scraping rather than stirring.

Cook the mixture to 260°F. It will be easier to keep the thermometer in a small pan, placing it in the mixture only occasionally and washing it with the pastry-brush. At 260°F., allow a few drops to run off the spatula into very cold water. When chilled, they should be capable of being moulded to a quite firm ball. Thermometers are sometimes slightly erratic when testing caramel after milk solids have been added, and this method of checking hardness is more reliable.

Dip the bottom of the pan in cold water to check the cooking and place it on a cool, heatproof surface. Stir in a teaspoonful of vanilla flavour. Pour the mixture out on the slab or in the tin to set, and when it is cool but not hard, score the surface by pressing the sharp edge of a knife into it, to mark bite-sized pieces.

For a caramel soft enough to be pulled and stretched, the final temperature could be 250°F., and for a harder one which will be fairly brittle but chewy, it could be 270°F. or more, although with these higher temperatures it would be wise to add the butter and condensed milk when the syrup has reached a higher temperature, say 265°F. or more. If milk solids are added at lower temperatures they have to be cooked that much longer before the final temperature is reached. This gives the caramel a much darker colour and causes loss of flavour. But whatever final temperature you choose, you should always check the hardness by dripping a little into very cold water or on a cold slab and testing it. If it is too hard, stir a little hot water into the boil and test again. In fact, caramels can be recooked even after they have been poured and allowed to set. If the hardened caramels are too hard or too soft, they can be chopped or broken up, put in a pan with a little water and reheated over a low light. The pan bottom must be scraped constantly because the caramel burns easily.

The quantities given in the Basic Caramel Recipe are easily varied, and one of the fascinating parts of sweet-making is substituting different quantities and ingredients to produce a different result. Instead of using 8 oz. granulated sugar use, say, 5 oz. granulated sugar and 3 oz. brown or Demerara sugar to obtain the distinctive raw sugar flavour. If this is not strong enough for your taste, use less granulated and more brown sugar. Brown sugars tend to curdle milk since they contain some acid. A little bicarbonate of soda dissolved in a little water will help by neutralising the acid, but if it does curdle it is not a catastrophe since it is hardly noticeable in the finished caramel. If you wish to make a more chewy caramel, use 8 oz. glucose powder instead of the 4 oz. given in the recipe. To make a superb rich creamy caramel, use up to 10 oz. full cream condensed milk and an extra ounce of butter with the same quantities of the other ingredients.

The best way is to work out a recipe first, based on the principles given in this chapter, and write it down before making a start. Indeed, it is a good practice to keep a note of everything you cook, including a description of the results, and in that way you can always repeat anything which particularly appeals to your taste.

By adding further ingredients to the basic caramel mixture many interesting variations can be made.

Chocolate Caramel: Stir in 2 oz. bitter eating chocolate, melted or chopped finely, at the end of the cooking process just before the caramel is to be poured out.

Coffee Caramel: Instant coffee can be used or a good liquid coffee essence such as 'Camp'. Three or four teaspoonfuls of either should be sufficient. The instant coffee should be dissolved in as little hot water as possible. Since the addition of either form of coffee will have the effect of softening the caramel, cook it a little harder, say 5°F. The coffee is stirred in at the end of the cooking process just before pouring out. Do not add vanilla essence.

Maple or Rum Caramel: Stir in one teaspoonful of maple or rum essence instead of the vanilla essence mentioned in the recipe.

Nut Caramel: Chop 2 oz. walnut pieces, brazil nuts or blanched almonds roughly and stir in just before pouring. Ideally, the nuts should be warmed before they are added. If they cool and thicken the caramel too much, it can be reheated slightly before pouring. A small piece of walnut or brazil nut can be placed on top of these caramels for decoration after they have been dipped in couverture.

Fruit Caramel: About 2 oz. currants can be stirred into the basic mix just before pouring. Again, they can be warmed beforehand so that the caramel does not cool and thicken too much. Small sultanas can be used as an alternative. After dipping, the caramels can be decorated with a currant.

Date, Fig or Cherry Caramel: Chop about 2 oz. dates, figs or glacé cherries, warm and stir into the basic mix just before pouring.

Ginger Caramel: Dry an ounce or two, depending on taste, of preserved stem ginger very carefully, chop into small pieces and warm slightly in a pan. Stir into the basic mix thoroughly so that any remaining syrup is well distributed in the caramel. Ginger caramels may be decorated with a small piece of crystallised ginger.

Honey Caramel: Stir in 5 or 6 teaspoonfuls of clear honey before pouring. Thick honey, being crystalline, makes the caramel cloudy although it does not make it grain since it is a form of invert sugar. As with the Coffee Caramel, this should be cooked at least 5°F. harder to compensate for the softening effect of the honey.

Reheating caramels after flavours, nuts or fruit have been added, causes loss of flavour and nuts and fruit tend to dry and harden, so if it has to be done, do it gently.

One great advantage of the basic caramel mixture is that you can make two or three times the quantity in one big pan. After cooking it to the correct degree, small quantities can be poured out into other pans and mixed with the various nuts, fruit and flavours before pouring on the slab. By this method, one boiling can yield a large variety of caramels. It is also possible to pour a soft caramel and then continue to cook the remaining quantity in the pan to a harder consistency.

I am sure many other flavours will occur to you and many other additions can be made. The important thing to remember about adding liquids is the softening effect it has on the final result. The more, or the thinner, the liquid, the harder must the caramel be cooked before it is added.

Personally, I do not feel that fruit flavours such as orange or lemon are always successful in a butter or creamy mixture. However, it is possible to make a caramel without butter or milk and the following recipe shows how.

Fruit-flavour Caramel

Equipment: Two 5-in. pans, thermometer, pastry-brush, greased slab and bars or tin set in cold water, scales.

Ingredients: 8 oz. granulated sugar
2 oz. powdered glucose
2 oz. flavourless vegetable fat such as Trex or Spry or a vegetable oil

½ teaspoonful gelatine powder soaked in a little water

concentrated fruit juice

tiny pinch citric acid dissolved in ½ teaspoonful water.

Method: Dissolve the sugar and glucose in 4 oz. water and cook to 240°F. in accordance with the sugar-boiling procedure. Add the vegetable fat or oil and the gelatine. Cook to 260°F. – no stirring is necessary since nothing will stick to the bottom of the pan and burn. Remove from the heat, check the cooking by dipping the pan in cold water for an instant. Add the citric acid, enough fruit juice to give a good flavour, and pour on the greased slab. The gelatine has to be added to ensure that the fat and syrup combine properly. If heated above 180°F., gelatine loses its ability to gel, but we are not using it for that purpose and its capacity to emulsify fat is not affected by higher temperatures. The citric acid, obtainable from any chemist, is to improve flavour and give it a little bite. This caramel has to be cooked harder to compensate for the fruit juice and also for the absence of milk solids which help the 'stand-up' qualities of caramels in which they are used.

Butterscotch

Butterscotch is simply a very hard caramel, easy to make, which blends well with a chocolate coating.

Equipment: Two 5-in. pans, thermometer, pastry-brush, greased slab and bars or tin set in cold water, scales.

Ingredients: 8 oz. granulated sugar
3 oz. powdered glucose
2 oz. butter
lemon oil or essence.

Method: Dissolve the sugar and glucose in sufficient water, 4 oz., and bring to the boil in accordance with the sugar-boiling procedure. Cook rapidly to 290–300°F., remembering that after 250°F. the thermometer travels very quickly indeed and has to be watched constantly. Remove from the heat and stir in the butter in pieces. There should be enough heat in the syrup to caramelise the butter sufficiently to give a good colour. If not, the pan can be returned to the heat for a few moments. Allow to cool before stirring in the lemon flavour. Pour between bars on a greased marble slab or into the tin.

A tasty variation is to add 2 oz. chopped toasted almonds. Almonds are blanched by putting them into cold water, bringing them to a strong boil, then draining them and adding cold water. A little pressure is exerted on the almonds between finger and thumb and the nut slips out of the skin quite easily. The almonds can be arranged on a tray and put in an oven to cook at 290–310°F. They are done when they can be cut through the centre and show a pale fawn colour all through, and may then be chopped roughly and spread out on the slab or in a tray and the butterscotch can be poured over them. It is unlikely that the butterscotch will come into contact with the surface of the slab and therefore it is not necessary to grease it; it would be possible to use a formica surface too, since it would not be touched by very hot syrup. This mixture should be turned over and cut before it has hardened. The pieces can be dipped with the nuts uppermost to give an attractive pattern.

Buttered Walnuts

A butterscotch mixture can be made as above, but using 6 oz. powdered glucose instead of only 3 oz. This is necessary to combat the extra risk of graining. The butterscotch is not poured out, but kept hot enough to remain liquid and each walnut half is dropped in and submerged with an ordinary household fork or a dipping fork. It is then picked out and placed on an oiled slab to set. When it has hardened, it can be dipped in chocolate or wrapped in cellophane. Brazil nuts and almonds can be treated in the same way and make a more convenient-sized mouthful.

Caramels

From the principles given so far, it will be quite easy to make up your own recipes for various kinds of caramels. For instance, suppose we have a shot at treacle toffee.

Treacle Toffee

A toffee is simply a caramel which has been cooked harder until it is chewy, but not so hard that it is as brittle as butterscotch.

Instead of 8 oz. granulated sugar as given in the basic caramel recipe use, say, 4 oz. granulated and 4 oz. brown sugar. This, together with 3 oz. treacle, should be adequate for flavour but more treacle could be used. In both the treacle and the brown sugar there is quite a lot of invert sugar already, but nevertheless we can keep the amount of glucose powder at 4 oz. since there is a lot of stirring involved and it is not a disadvantage to have the toffee reasonably chewy or long-lasting. Condensed milk and butter can remain at 6 oz. and 2 oz. The butter is used to provide the fat content, and although condensed milk is optional and will almost certainly curdle from the acid in the brown sugar and treacle, it gives a good flavour. Lastly, a little lemon flavour would be pleasant. Therefore we have the following recipe:

> 4 oz. granulated sugar
> 4 oz. brown sugar
> 3 oz. treacle
> 6 oz. full cream sweetened condensed milk
> 4 oz. glucose powder
> 2 oz. fresh or lightly salted butter
> 1 teaspoonful lemon flavour.

The method would be to dissolve the sugar and glucose in water, say 4 oz., and bring to the boil. Treacle toffee is hard, but not brittle, so a final temperature of 270–275°F. should be adequate. Therefore, the condensed milk and butter should be warmed separately and added when the temperature has reached about 265°F. so that it does not have to cook too long. The treacle can be added later to preserve the flavour, then the whole mixture is brought to the final temperature, cooled slightly for the lemon flavour to be added, then poured on a marble slab.

If you prefer not to use milk because it curdles, use an extra ounce or so of butter instead to make up the fat content.

5

Fudge and Candy

Fudge

Fudge is rumoured to have been invented by chance, when a batch of caramel being made by students at an American college accidentally grained. From what has been said in earlier chapters, it is possible to guess what went wrong: either they stirred the mixture too much for the amount of doctoring agent used, or some crystalline substance got into the mixture.

The story, whether true or not, is useful to remember since it emphasises that fudge is simply a caramel encouraged to grain. Therefore, any of the recipes given for caramel are suitable for making fudge, but the quantity of the doctoring agent can be reduced a little to the point at which grain is merely controlled to a fine crystal rather than being inhibited altogether.

There are, as explained already, two methods of encouraging grain; agitation and seeding. Seeding consists of introducing some crystalline substance into the boil at the end of the cooking process. This substance may be icing sugar, fondant or anything with a similar structure. Grain by agitation can be caused by stirring or beating the mixture while in the pan, rubbing the back of the spoon on the side of the pan until a small quantity begins to cloud, or pouring the mixture out on to a slab and stirring or folding it there.

The other notable difference between fudge and caramel is that fudge is cooked to a lower temperature. This gives a softer, more moist result, and whereas caramel cooked to this lower temperature would still be liquid, the crystalline structure of fudge makes it stand up. The recipe given here is cooked to 240°F., but you could increase the final temperature to 250°F. for a harder fudge.

To illustrate the similarity between caramels and fudge, we can take the basic Caramel Recipe given in the last chapter and turn it into a fudge recipe.

Basic Fudge Recipe

Equipment: 6-in. pan, 5-in. pan, thermometer, small saucepan, scales, wooden or marble slab and iron bars or rectangular tin, pastry-brush, silicone paper, wooden spatula.

Ingredients: 8 oz. granulated sugar or 5 oz. brown and 3 oz.
          granulated
      4 oz. glucose powder
      2 oz. lightly salted butter
      6 oz. full cream sweetened condensed milk
      vanilla flavour.

Method: The procedure for sugar-boiling should be followed except that there will be three pans in use, with the extra one for pre-mixing the butter and the condensed milk.

Fudge should not be poured directly on to marble or tin but these should be lined with oiled greaseproof paper or silicone paper. The latter, sold as 'Bakewell Paper', is much simpler to use. There is no problem about this since fudge is fairly cool when it is poured out, and when it has set the paper peels off quite easily. Indeed, a wooden board can be used with your iron bars, provided both are lined with silicone paper.

This step-by-step method of making fudge should ensure there are no mistakes.

1. Assemble the equipment listed above. Line the tin or slab and bars with silicone paper. Fudge is normally poured deeper than caramel and this recipe will pour a block about

8 x 6 in. and ⅜ in. deep, so the bars should be arranged to that size.

2. Weigh out the sugar and glucose in the large pan and add enough water to dissolve them, i.e. 3 oz. or a little more. Weigh the butter and condensed milk into the other pan and put the thermometer into the third pan and add water.

3. Heat all three pans, stirring the sugar constantly to dissolve it thoroughly and bring it to the boil. Allow the butter and condensed milk to melt gently, preferably over hot water rather than direct heat, since it goes lumpy if heated too quickly. Bring the other pan to the boil, keeping the thermometer in, and check the temperature.

4. Boil the syrup to 240°F. Add the butter and milk and, stirring constantly with a wooden spatula, preferably one with a straight edge along the bottom, bring it back to 240°F. By this time, the mixture should have a nice brown colour.

5. Remove the pan from the heat and check the boiling by dipping the base of the pan in water. Allow the bubbles to subside then beat vigorously with the wooden spatula for a minute or so until the mixture just begins to cloud. Add the vanilla and pour out on the slab or tin, adding the final scrapings from the pan. If the fudge has thickened too much to pour easily, reheat it gently until it is quite liquid. After pouring, allow to cool and then score with a greased knife.

The fudge may look more like caramel after it has been poured, but as it cools, the graining, induced by beating, will gradually work its way throughout the block.

The 'seeding' method of graining is, if anything, even easier than the beating method. After the mixture has been removed from the heat and the bubbles have ceased, stir in a rounded dessertspoonful of sieved icing sugar – there must be no lumps in the icing sugar – then pour it in the usual way. The advantage of this method is that you are absolutely certain it will grain, although it may be a little coarse. With the other method, it is more difficult for the inexperienced to be sure the mixture has been beaten sufficiently. Fondant can be used instead of icing sugar, 1 oz. would be sufficient, added in small pieces and this gives a much finer grain.

Some authorities believe fudge must not be poured on a cold surface or it will produce a spotty effect. It is also believed that a finer grain is achieved if beating is commenced after the mixture has cooled to 150°F. In my experience, the temperature at which beating commences is irrelevant, but the fudge must be very liquid, and therefore quite hot, when it is poured and this gives a smooth, clear, unspotted surface.

All the variations on the basic caramel recipe can be used for fudges, but the amount of glucose is fairly constant. In caramels, more glucose can be used to give a more chewy texture, which is not needed in fudge. You can use brown sugar instead of granulated to get the raw sugar flavour. Although there is some acid in brown sugar, condensed milk seems less liable to curdle and it would be hardly noticed anyway. A very rich creamy fudge can be made by using 10 oz. condensed milk instead of 6 oz., and 3 oz. butter instead of 2 oz. Many other variations on the basic fudge recipe are possible.

Chocolate Fudge: Stir in 2 oz. melted or chopped chocolate just before beating the mixture.

Coffee Fudge: The mixture should be cooked a little harder, say 245°F. Allow it to cool before stirring in 3 or 4 teaspoonfuls of coffee essence or instant coffee dissolved in a little water. The mixture can then be beaten.

Honey Fudge: Cook the fudge to 245°F. then beat until it grains. Finally add 2 or 3 rounded teaspoonfuls of honey, either clear or thick. If the honey is added before the mixture is beaten, being a form of invert sugar it helps to prevent granulation. The mixture can be warmed again, if necessary, before it is poured.

Maple or Rum Fudge. Stir in a teaspoonful of maple or rum essence before commencing to beat.

Nut Fudge: About 2 oz. of nuts, either walnuts, brazil nuts or blanched almonds, can be chopped roughly, warmed and either stirred in at the end of the beating process or the fudge can be poured and the nuts sprinkled on the surface and then pressed in a little, perhaps with a rolling-pin.

Fruit Fudge: About 2 oz. currants or sultanas, with or without a little mixed peel, can be warmed and added to the mixture after beating.

Date, Fig or Cherry Fudge: Chop about 2 oz. dates, figs or glacé cherries, warm and stir in after beating. Cherries could, alternatively, be pressed into the surface of the fudge after it has been poured.

Ginger Fudge: Dry an ounce or so of preserved stem ginger, chop and mix it in thoroughly after beating the mixture.

Of course, you could make a mixture. Nuts, as well as fruit, including glacé cherries, can be added. Moreover, these could be added to a coffee or a chocolate fudge instead of a vanilla fudge. The combinations and permutations are endless, just go ahead and experiment and do not worry too much about it going wrong. After all, fudge was a caramel which went wrong.

COLOURS AND FLAVOURS

Before discussing candy, it is necessary to have a look at colours and flavours since they are very important in making candy and in many of the other centres described in later chapters.

Flavours for sweets are not an easy problem for the home chocolatier, and the professional has the advantage of being able to obtain first-class concentrates and essences of a wide variety of fruits which are not available on the domestic market. Actual fruit juices are not the best for making sweets. Lemon juice, for instance, is too watery and would thin down any centre to which it was added, also the flavour of lemon is in the zest rather than in the juice. However, professional chocolatiers do not always use the best products which are available to them because they are often extremely expensive and substitutes are used which do not have the same fresh flavours.

Boots sell lemon spirit, orange compound and peppermint oil which, even in minute quantities, give the real scent and flavour of the fruits and herb from which they are derived. The first two are very expensive, but the peppermint oil is essential for chocolate making although still quite expensive. Boots also sell clove oil, which is used more for toothache than for flavouring.

For home sweet-making, concentrated orange juice is widely available. Sunquick make concentrated lemon and orange juices which are quite suitable for chocolate centres. Both may be improved by the addition of a little citric acid, available at any chemist's, to give more bite, and some grated lemon or orange peel. Whenever a lemon or an orange is being used in the kitchen, the peel can be grated and kept in a polythene bag in the deep-freeze for later use. Sunquick also make concentrated tangerine and grapefruit which are quite good. Deep-frozen tinned concentrates are available of orange, lemon and grapefruit juice, and these are also successful. Certainly, any of these concentrates are better than the chemical flavours sold in little bottles at the grocers. Still, even these are sometimes quite useful on their own, and can often be used to supplement and strengthen a fruit concentrate.

Raspberries are now available throughout the year either fresh or frozen. They can be squashed through a sieve with the back of a spoon. Done properly, it is laborious work and everything should be pressed through except the pips. This purée gives excellent flavour but it may make a centre too dark in colour, and this has to be corrected by the addition of some red food colour. Cochineal is much too dark for this purpose. The flavour of the purée can also be improved by the addition of a little citric acid.

Jams are a form of concentrated fruit, but they are not often very successful for our purpose since they taste like jam. However, you may find a suitable fresh fruit preserve, and a little citric acid could freshen it even more.

Strawberry is a popular flavour which should always be made from fresh or frozen fruit puréed in a blender, or, if necessary, mashed with a fork. Icing sugar can be dissolved into the purée to thicken it if necessary.

Apricot flavour can be made from the dried fruit, soaked overnight and then softened by cooking it in a little sugar syrup. It should then be puréed in a blender or pressed through a sieve. You may find apricot jam more successful than other jams.

The object is to get the most flavour into the least amount of liquid, so that when it is added to a syrup or a fondant it thins it down as little as possible. Fruit concentrates and purées should not, as far as possible, be added to excessively hot liquids since flavours are volatile and can easily evaporate or be weakened. Indeed, if you can smell any essence, it is because it is evaporating, and if it is evaporating, it is becoming weaker.

The colour of a centre is a very important clue to its flavour, and quite often, having got the flavour right in a sweet, the colour may be wrong, as with raspberries, or the colour may be rather weak and need strengthening. Food colours on sale now are carefully controlled and quite safe. It would be useful to obtain a small bottle of each of the following colours: red, yellow, green, orange and violet, which should serve most of your needs and can be used in combination. Red and violet, for instance, give a blackberry colour. Some colours are traditionally associated with particular flavours, and if the colour is wrong for the flavour it simply confuses people and the sweet does not taste right. You might find this list of colours and their associated flavours quite helpful.

Pale yellow – lemon, pineapple
Orange – orange
Green – lime, almond, peppermint
White – vanilla, almond, peppermint
Pink – strawberry, rose
Red – raspberry.

Having looked at flavours and colours, we can make some candy.

Candy

Candy is a coarser-grained confection than fudge and to achieve this, less glucose is used. It is also harder than fudge and there-fore must be cooked to a higher temperature, say 250°F. or more. The third difference is that candy rarely contains any fat. It is often given fruit flavours such as orange, lemon or rasp-berry, but any flavour can be used. It is not often dipped in chocolate since fondant is the more usual base for fruit flavours for dipping. Nevertheless, a few pieces, in various colours, can help enormously to brighten up the look of a box of chocolates.

The recipe for Orange Candy is another basic recipe which can be used for many other flavours.

Orange Candy

Equipment: 6-in. pan, 5-in. pan, thermometer, pastry-brush, scales, wooden or marble slab and bars or rectangular tin lined with silicone paper.

Ingredients: 12 oz. granulated sugar
1 oz. glucose powder
pinch citric acid dissolved in a little water
2 tablespoonfuls orange concentrate
1 teaspoonful grated orange peel
1 dessertspoonful sieved icing sugar.

Method: The sugar and glucose are dissolved in a little water, say 4 oz., by heating and stirring. Less glucose is used in order to encourage a coarser grain. The citric acid, although itself a doctor, does not affect the amount of glucose since it is being used for flavour, not for controlling grain, and is therefore added at the end of cooking.

Cook the syrup rapidly to 255°F. and then check the boil by dipping the base of the pan into water for a moment. Add the citric acid and the orange concentrate and orange peel, then stir in the icing sugar. Pour out the mixture on the silicone paper to a depth of about ¾ in. This quantity will make a slab about 5 x 5 in. The mixture will be very liquid when it is poured, but will grain gradually as it cools and hardens. Score the surface in bite-sized pieces with a greased knife.

The other flavours described earlier can be used instead of orange. If peppermint oil or ground ginger is used, the candy could be cooked to 250°F. only. The higher temperature given in the recipe takes account of the thinning effect of the concentrate. Peppermint candy can be coloured green or left white, and the peppermint oil must be added with an eye-dropper.

After it has set, candy looks extremely attractive with the sugar crystals catching the light and giving sparkle to the bright and cheerful colours. If you have ever visited Rye in Sussex, you must have noticed that one of its unique features is the way the old tea-shops vie with each other in offering a most delightful selection of fudges and candies.

6

Fondant

Fondant was invented in the middle of the last century and soon became extremely important in chocolate-making. It is the basis of all the 'creams': strawberry creams, coffee creams, peppermint creams, rose and violet creams and so on. From a third to a half of the chocolates in most boxes are likely to be made from fondant.

Following the instructions for sugar-boiling, fondant is simple to make and the only ingredients are granulated sugar, a doctoring agent and water. These are mixed to a syrup and cooked to a temperature of 240–245°F. The syrup is poured out on to a cold surface and encouraged to cool as quickly as possible. It is then grained by agitation, and soon after it clouds and thickens it sets quite hard. The pieces are picked up and squeezed when they break down and become plastic and soft. The fondant should be left in an airtight box for a day or two to mature. The best fondant is very white, soft and with a fine grain.

Fondant can be reheated, flavoured and thinned down, if necessary with a little sugar and water syrup. It can then be poured on a slab in the form of discs, piped through a forcing bag into various shapes, or poured into depressions made by moulds in trays filled with cornflour. The fondant solidifies and becomes hard enough to handle for the purpose of dipping in chocolate. To obtain the soft flowing creams, an enzyme called invertase is added to the fondant before it is poured, and this inverts the sugar further after it has been coated with chocolate. Therefore, after a fortnight or so, the centre can become quite liquid, depending on the amount of invertase used.

Fondant is widely used by confectioners for icing cakes and buns and they have no difficulty in obtaining it ready-made from their suppliers. The manufactured product is at least as good as the best hand-made fondant and if you can persuade your confectioner to sell you a quantity you will save yourself some hard work – I have never been so lucky.

The difference between fondant and icing sugar is that while icing sugar is finely ground granulated sugar, fondant contains a proportion of invert sugar. In the confectionery trade, fondant can be obtained in powder form and I have no doubt that this is just as effective. In fact, on occasions, I have used ordinary icing sugar for making fondant centres, and also a mixture of icing sugar and glucose powder in the proportions of three parts of icing sugar to one of glucose. Adding a small quantity of liquid gives a consistency very similar to fondant but it is very coarse-grained.

A fondant centre made only from icing sugar and water or a flavouring liquid would rapidly dry out leaving it hard and brittle. The addition of glucose makes it softer and more moist and if invertase is added to an icing sugar centre, with or without glucose, it is difficult to anyone but an expert to tell the difference from fondant. The snag is that icing sugar is very expensive, and if it gets damp it must be sieved to remove the lumps. But there is no reason why you should not use icing sugar if you cannot buy fondant and don't want to make it.

How to Make Fondant

Equipment: 6-in. pan, 5-in. pan for the thermometer, scales, pastry-brush and a metal spoon. You will also need a slab on which to pour out the hot syrup.

If you have a marble slab that will be ideal, but a formica-covered board or table top is quite suitable since the temperature of the syrup will not be so high that the formica will be damaged.

A slab 14 in. square will be quite large enough for the quantity given in the recipe. However, larger quantities can be made, using a larger slab or using iron bars. In any case, the slab should be wiped down with a cold wet cloth just before pouring the syrup, to help cool it quickly. You will also need an implement to scrape the thick syrup off the surface of the slab. The ideal tool is one used for scraping off wallpaper which has a rigid V-shaped blade – one 4 in. wide is just about right. A fried egg server, known as a 'slotted turner', which looks like a spade but with an angled flexible blade, can be used but it will not last long; the blade will eventually crack at the point where it is attached to the handle. Also, you will need a knife or flexible metal spatula for scraping the syrup off the scraper. Lastly, it is useful to have a basin of water handy in which to dip the base of the pan to check the boil.

Ingredients: 14 oz. granulated sugar
2 oz. glucose powder
4 oz. water.

The quantity of water, one-quarter the combined weight of the sugar and glucose, is just enough to dissolve all the sugar and glucose just before the mixture begins to boil. More water can be used but it makes the boiling process longer, since it has to be evaporated before the desired temperature can be reached. The quantity of glucose is, in my experience, just about right for the amount of sugar. There must be enough glucose to control grain and to prevent it from becoming too coarse, but not so much that it takes an excessive amount of stirring to make it grain. Using these proportions, the syrup can be made to cream in about 10 minutes: using 3 oz. glucose to 14 oz. sugar can take over 20 minutes' work, and the result is no better.

Method: Following the sugar-boiling procedure, the small pan is filled with water and put on to boil with the thermometer in. When it reaches the boil the temperature must be 212°F.

80

Fondant

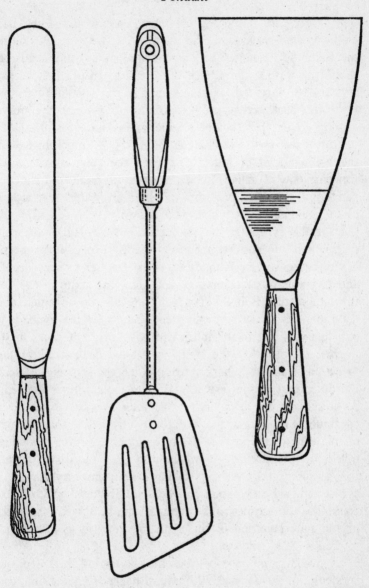

Fondant Tools

The larger pan, containing the sugar, glucose and water, is put on heat and stirred with the metal spoon – a wooden one may discolour the fondant. The sides of the pan and the metal spoon should be washed down with the brush to ensure that all sugar crystals are dissolved. If necessary, the pan should be removed from the heat and stirring continued to prevent the mixture coming to the boil before all the grains have dissolved. This mixture will come to the boil at about 225°F., much higher than the boiling point of water (212°F.) since there is such a high concentration of sugar. Cook the syrup to 242°F., remove the pan from the heat and dip the base in water to check the cooking and allow the bubbles to die down.

Pour the syrup on the slab, previously wiped down with a damp cloth. Do not attempt to get the last drops out of the pan. Sprinkle the surface with drops of cold water to speed cooling and to prevent a skin forming, and allow the syrup to cool until the temperature is below 150°F. This will probably take about 5 minutes; the faster the syrup cools, the finer the grain. It will still feel very hot to the touch and will burn if it sticks to your fingers. If you allow the syrup to get too cool, it takes longer to cream it and it is harder work. Take the scraper and scrape the outer part of the pool of syrup and pour it over the centre. As it spreads out again, bring the outer part to the centre and continue working it in this way until you can see that the syrup on the edge of the scraper has turned white. Scrape this off and mix it in with the rest, it will help to grain the whole batch. If this scraping and turning is taking a long time, try stirring the syrup with a heavy spoon and beating air bubbles into it. You could use the scraper, but be careful not to scratch the surface of the slab. Aeration of the syrup in this way is also reputed to produce a finer crystal.

Eventually, the syrup will become cloudy and thick and, quite suddenly, it will set hard. How hard depends on the final cooking temperature. Pick up the pieces and squeeze them in your hands and they will soften and become plastic. Do not worry about individual little lumps, they will soften later. The fondant should be put in an airtight container and kept for a day or two at least. During this time it will, apparently, become more moist and soft. If left too long exposed to the air, it will dry out and become hard and difficult to use.

If the worst happened, and the syrup positively refused to grain, perhaps because it had cooled too much, you could always re-cook the syrup, adding the same amount of water as given in the recipe. As a last resort, you could even mix in a dessert-spoonful of sifted icing sugar and let it stand to see what happens. If the grain is very coarse it does not matter quite so much, because the enzyme invertase, which will be added to the fondant, will break the crystals down. However, a fine crystal is important if you intend to make a drier centre.

Fondant can be cooked to a final temperature anywhere between 238 and 248°F. Below 238°F. it is very runny and may not set. Above 248°F. it is very difficult to stir the thick syrup on the slab. However, some chocolatiers used to prefer a harder fondant because it allowed them to add more liquid flavouring without it thinning too much. I find 242°F. satisfactory for most purposes, although to be absolutely accurate it should be 244°F. in warm wet weather to obtain the same consistency.

THE STARCH TRAY

A starch tray is a valuable, indeed an essential piece of equipment for the home chocolatier. It is filled with cornflour and the prepared fondant is poured into depressions made in the cornflour. Cornflour is important because it will not absorb a concentrated sugar solution. In addition, it is edible, so that any minute quantities adhering to the fondants can be ignored. It absorbs a certain amount of moisture from the fondant, helping to make a hard crust which can withstand handling. Cornflour can also be used over and over again, and lastly, it retains the impression of a mould accurately.

Cornflour must be sieved occasionally to take out odd drops of fondant which might have accidentally dripped. It should be baked occasionally in the oven to kill off any germs or spores which may have infected it, and it should be dried out from time to time at a low temperature in the oven to restore its capacity to absorb moisture.

Trays suitable for use as starch trays can be bought at garden shops. Made of plastic, they are available in various sizes but the disadvantage is they are a little small and you would need more than one. Alternatively, a starch tray may be made from an old drawer, which has the advantage of being solidly constructed, or from any wooden box. It should be $1\frac{1}{2}$ in. deep at least, but should not be more than 2 in deep since this increases the amount of cornflour required, which has all to be kept clean and dry. A drawer can have a false bottom put in. A do-it-yourself shop will sell you a piece of $\frac{3}{4}$ in. plywood cut to size and some blocks of wood of the right thickness. The blocks can be glued to the base of the drawer and the plywood glued on top of them. The gap between the plywood and the sides of the drawer can be covered with sticky paper. The size of the tray or drawer is up to you, but mine is $15\frac{1}{4}$ x $17\frac{1}{4}$ in. inside measurement and I find it adequate. It is large enough to cast 90 peppermint creams of $1\frac{1}{4}$ in. diameter or 130 smaller centres. If this is not enough, it may be easier to make more than one tray rather than have one very large one, but in this case it would be best to have them the same size so that the same moulds will fit them all. Mine is also $1\frac{3}{4}$ in. deep and holds about 8 lb. cornflour, which will give an idea of the quantity of cornflour required. You must decide where you are going to put the tray while you are using it, and also where you can store it. If you have bought a whole wash-stand, including marble top and drawer, you can simply slide the drawer back in its place.

You will also need some lengths of wood, each one cut a little longer than the width of your starch tray. By 'width' I mean the distance from right to left when the tray is in position ready for use. These lengths should be $\frac{7}{8}$ in. by $\frac{1}{2}$ in. thick and ordinary deal, planed all round will be quite adequate. One length will be needed to smooth over the surface of the cornflour until you have it completely level with the sides of the tray. If it is difficult to smooth and it makes lumps, the cornflour is probably too damp and it should be dried out.

The other lengths of wood will have moulds glued to them which will be pressed into the cornflour to make the depressions which will later be filled with fondant.

MOULDS AND HOW TO MAKE THEM

Starch moulds can be purchased, they are not easy to obtain but are supplied by Errington & Sons, Rodney Road, Southsea, Portsmouth, Hants. I prefer larger ones than are normally available commercially, and make them myself. The sort of material required for this has the consistency of clay so that it can be

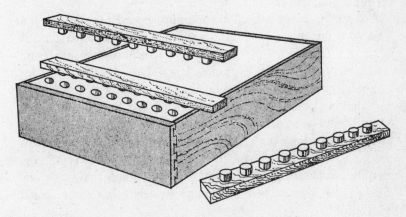

Starch Tray and Moulds

moulded to shape, and the characteristic of setting very hard with as little shrinkage as possible, nor should it crumble or disintegrate. Neither plaster of Paris nor clay is satisfactory. However, there are several modelling compounds stocked by shops which specialise in artists' materials, which can be used. 'Superwood' is a powder to which water is added to produce a consistency like clay. It can be dried in a few hours in the oven, when it becomes hard and assumes the texture of wood and can be carved or sandpapered like wood. It is not messy to use.

'Sofenbak' is another modelling compound. The instructions for mixing it must be followed exactly, but the compound sets rock-hard. It can be messy to work and the hands must be kept damp, otherwise the Sofenbak sticks and as it dries it forms an unpleasant crust, but this washes off without difficulty. After Sofenbak has hardened it can be broken up, treated in accordance with the instructions and used again. Drying takes several days, but normal room temperatures should give a crust hard enough for our purpose within 24 hours. When drying any of these materials, it is important to turn them over after a time to ensure that they dry all round. Sofenbak and Superwood both shrink about one sixth per inch on drying, Superwood perhaps shrinks a little more than Sofenbak.

A compound called 'Das' has recently appeared on the market. This is ready mixed and only needs moulding. I understand it is not messy to use and there is very little shrinkage, therefore it would appear to be quite suitable for moulds.

The compounds can be moulded to any shape with the fingers, and ideas for shapes can be obtained from any box of chocolates. Some shapes are particularly associated with individual flavours and you may wish to follow the same patterns since it helps people to recognise them. It should be remembered that the moulds have to be made a little smaller than you wish the finished chocolate to be since the cast fondant has to be coated with chocolate.

Two popular shapes are a disc and a drum. The discs, which I use for peppermint creams, can be cut $1\frac{1}{4}$ in. in diameter and $\frac{3}{8}$ in. deep; and drums, which I use for all other creams, can be 1 in. diameter and $\frac{1}{2}$ in. or $\frac{7}{16}$ in. deep. The actual moulds will be slightly smaller when they have dried out, through shrinkage. They can be stamped out very accurately if the compound is first rolled out like pastry, with a rolling-pin or milk bottle, using a dusting of dry compound to prevent sticking. When the compound has been rolled to the correct thickness, the shapes can be pressed out with metal cutters. It is possible to buy a straight-edged or 'plain' pastry-cutter of $1\frac{1}{4}$ in diameter, but a 1 in. cutter will be more difficult to obtain and is more likely to be found in a set of vegetable cutters. Creeds (see p. 149) should be able to help, or G. F. and H. J. Mathews Co. Ltd., 214/6, Borough High Street, London S.E.1, carry an excellent range of kitchen ware and have a tinsmith's attached to the shop which can make tools and utensils to order.

Alternatively, it is not difficult to make cutters from used tin cans provided you can use a soldering iron. With a tin-opener, cut out both ends of the tin, and with an ordinary pair of household scissors, cut down the side of the tin near the join and

Empty tin can

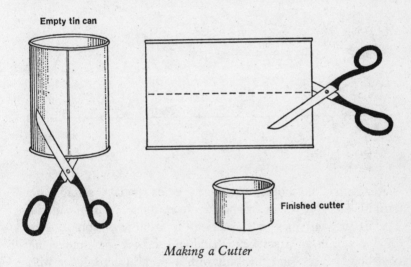

Finished cutter

Making a Cutter

unroll it. Cut along the tin between the reinforced rims; the distance from the rim determines the depth of the cutter, $1\frac{1}{2}$–$2\frac{1}{2}$ in. from the rim should be enough. The sharp edge is for cutting and the reinforced rim should be retained for safety, since the hand presses down on it. The tin can be bent round a pipe with a little tapping with a hammer to give the desired diameter, making allowance for $\frac{1}{8}$ in. overlap, then cut off the excess. Cut off $\frac{1}{4}$ in. of the reinforced rim to make a neat join and solder the join, trying not to have a gap at the overlap or it will not cut a perfect circle. Final adjustments can be made to the shape of the cutter after it has been soldered, since the tin is not too thick to be squeezed to shape in the fingers. If you wanted a mould with a smaller diameter, say $\frac{7}{8}$ in., wine bottle corks are adequate and quite cheap.

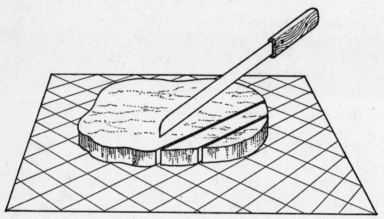

Cutting Diamond-shaped Moulds

A diamond is another useful shape for moulds, suitable for Turkish Delight, which can be cut $\frac{7}{16}$ in. thick and 1 in. square. The easiest and most accurate way to cut these moulds is to draw a pattern on paper beforehand and roll out some modelling compound on top and then cut with a knife in accordance with the pattern.

After the moulds have hardened, they can be glued on to the lengths of wood mentioned earlier, with any of the usual kinds of glue. There should be a space of not less than $\frac{5}{8}$ in. between each mould to ensure good impressions, and you will have to make sure there is sufficient space at each end of the length to allow the end moulds to keep clear of the sides of the starch tray. There should be enough moulds of each shape to fill two separate lengths of wood. After the cornflour has been smoothed out in the tray, the first set of moulds are pressed into the cornflour and they are left in while the second set are pressed in alongside. Then the first set is removed and pressed in next to the second set, and so on, leap-frogging down the tray. The reason for this is that when a length of moulds is pressed into the cornflour, there is some disturbance which can push the other depressions out of shape. Keeping one length of moulds in the tray while another length is pressed in, ensures that the depressions are not affected by this movement.

When the moulds are being withdrawn from the cornflour, the length should be held at both ends and can be fractionally moved from side to side to make the hole a little larger. This ensures that when the moulds are lifted, there is less risk of their collapsing the sides of the depressions.

PREPARING AND CASTING FONDANT

Fondant can be piped through a forcing bag but the variety of shapes is limited and a great deal of practice is needed to obtain consistency of size.

Stencil mats can be purchased, made of rubber, which have various shapes moulded in. The hot fondant is poured into the spaces and allowed to cool; the mat is then bent back and the fondants should pop out. Mats are very expensive, however, one mat is needed for each shape and there are not many shapes available. Moreover, if the fondant is a little thin when it is poured, the excess moisture will not evaporate as the rubber is not absorbent, therefore the fondant will stick inside the moulds. This means having to scrape the fondant out, washing and drying the mat and starting again.

A third method is to pour out discs of fondant which, when hardened, can be either dipped in chocolate or eaten as they are. For this purpose, the fondant should be heated in a saucepan set in hot water. The fondant should not be heated above 125°F. or its appearance may be affected, but if these centres are to be chocolate-coated, the temperature can be increased to 165°F. Flavour should be added, peppermint oil is particularly effective, but coffee, orange or lemon concentrates are very good. The consistency should be like a thick cream, but if it is too thick, water can be added in very tiny amounts, or better still, dissolve some sugar in a little warm water and add some of that. When the fondant is thoroughly mixed, remove the pan from the hot water, carefully drying the bottom of the pan to prevent drips. The fondant should not be poured on a very cold surface but on silicone paper. The pan should be held in one hand with a tablespoon in the other to catch any drips, and the fondant can be poured to make discs $1\frac{1}{2}$ in. in diameter. If they have a little peak in the middle, the fondant is too cool or too thick.

The dipping process for these discs is a little different from that for other chocolates. They should be dropped on the surface of the tempered couverture, lifted out with a four-pronged fork and overturned on the silicone or wax paper, fondant-side down. When the couverture has set, the half-dipped fondants are again dropped on the surface of the couverture to coat the other side. Again, the fondant is lifted out with the four-pronged fork and overturned on the paper. This ensures that the mark of the prongs appears on both sides.

Fondant can also be moulded in the fingers like truffles, and then coated with couverture. It must first be melted in a pan set in hot water, the fondant temperature should not exceed 165°F. or the crystals will thicken. The flavours can be added and the fondant allowed to cool, it is then stirred to restore its plasticity and pieces can be pulled off and pressed to any desired shape. The hands can be dusted with icing sugar to prevent sticking. If the fondants are then put on one side on a tray dusted with a little cornflour, the outside will dry out, forming a crust. The fondants should be turned over to allow them to harden all round. They should now be firm enough to withstand dipping in couverture and the insides will remain soft and moist.

Although, admittedly, it takes some time to make or purchase the necessary equipment, which can be irritating, there is no doubt that the most interesting, quickest and least risky way of making fondants is by casting them in cornflour. The equipment mentioned so far comprises the starch tray filled with dried cornflour, one length of wood for making the surface of the cornflour level with the edge of the starch tray, and two lengths for each shape of mould. One other item is essential and a further one is extremely useful. The essential one is a flour sieve with a wooden rim. I prefer a nylon mesh, and a 9-in. sieve should be large enough. It should not be difficult to obtain one from any supplier of kitchen equipment. The optional item is a fondant funnel. This is a heavy, tin, V-shaped funnel with a handle at the side, but it does not have a long spout like most funnels. Instead, it has a reinforced copper end with a narrow hole. Mine is $6\frac{1}{2}$ in. across the top, $8\frac{1}{2}$ in. deep with a $\frac{3}{8}$-in. hole at the bottom. They can be purchased from G. F. and H. J. Mathews (see p. 149). You will also need a piece of dowel or the handle of a wooden spoon, which is put inside the funnel and must be thick enough just to block the hole.

The necessary ingredients include the fondant, the flavourings discussed in detail in the last chapter, some stock syrup and some invertase.

Stock Syrup: The stock syrup is needed just in case it is necessary to thin down the fondant. Plain water can be used in tiny quantities but is very drastic. Using sugar syrup means it is unnecessary to be quite so precise. Stock syrup is made from granulated sugar and water in the proportions of 2 parts sugar to 1 of water. For instance, 2 level tablespoonfuls of sugar and 1 of water should be put in a small saucepan and heated and stirred until the sugar is completely dissolved. This can then be put on one side until required.

Invertase: Invertase is extremely important in fondants since it produces those flowing moist centres and also acts as a preservative. Invertase is an enzyme produced by the yeast cell, and when added to cane sugar (which is known chemically as 'sucrose') invertase 'inverts' it; that is, it turns the sucrose into approximately equal amounts of two other sugars – 'levulose'

Making Chocolates

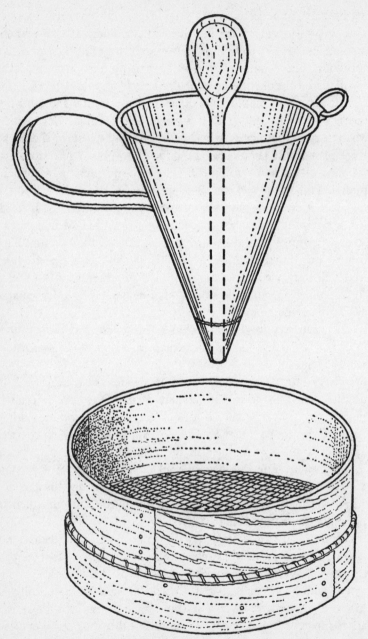

Flour Sieve and Fondant Funnel

and 'dextrose' which cannot form crystals. In effect, therefore, invertase liquefies cane sugar, but this takes place gradually over a period of time depending on how much is used. This action is inhibited by alkali, and therefore in hard-water areas a little acid, such as citric, should be added to the fondant to act as a neutraliser. Levulose and dextrose attract moisture – they are very hygroscopic – and when fondant containing invertase is put inside a chocolate coating, thus sealing it from the atmosphere, the invertase gradually turns the fondant into these two other sugars which then absorb all the moisture which may be in the centre. This effect is important, since any wild yeasts which might get into the fondant can cause fermentation, but only if they can find water. The invert sugar absorbs all the moisture available and prevents fermentation or mould developing. Chocolates cracking through a build-up of pressure inside caused by fermentation used to be a major problem for chocolatiers.

Invertase can be produced by a commercial process which separates it from the yeast cells and purifies it. It is manufactured under the brand names 'Liquine' by Food Industries Ltd., Bromborough Port, New Ferry, Birkenhead, Cheshire; and 'Sucrovert', made by the SuCrest Corporation, 120 Wall Street, New York, NY 10005. SuCrest also manufacture a double-strength invertase as well as a wide range of other products for the baking and confectionery trade including 'Nulofond', a dry fondant specially made for sweets. Invertase is normally only available in fairly large quantities; however, SuCrest pack a 1-lb. container, and although that is almost enough to treat half-a-ton of sugar, it is not expensive and keeps well in a cool place. A sample bottle would be enough to last quite a long time.

It is certainly well worth trying to obtain a supply, perhaps your confectioner will be prepared to help. If it is quite impossible to obtain, invertase can be produced at home, unfortunately not in so concentrated and purified a form, nor is its strength so predictable.

Invertase Recipe

Ingredients: 1 teaspoonful dried yeast pellets
1½ tablespoonfuls boiling water
1 teaspoonful granulated sugar.

Method: Dissolve the sugar in the hot water and add the yeast. Make sure the yeast is well broken up and allow it to stand, preferably in a warm place overnight. The mixture will froth as the yeast produces gas from absorbing the sugar. If allowed to cool, the mixture will stop working and separate into a clear liquid with a grey sediment. The separation can be helped by adding a little more water, since the yeast will have reproduced and grown overnight and some of the water will have evaporated.

Yeast water can be used stirred up, or the clear liquid can be skimmed off and used on its own. What is important is the amount of invertase, and this appears to be the same for the clear liquid as for the grey sediment. For peppermint or vanilla creams which use white fondant, it is best to use the clarified yeast water, since the grey yeast cells discolour. Added to other coloured fondants, however, it makes little difference.

Half a dessertspoonful, or ¼ fl. oz. to be exact, should be sufficient to add to 1 lb. fondant. This quantity will produce a moist centre within two weeks if the chocolates are kept at room temperature. If a very liquid centre is required, use 1 or 1½ dessertspoonfuls.

The instructions given here produce a fairly strong invertase solution. It is possible to make yeast water from ordinary concentrated yeast, but you would have to use twice as much, i.e. 2 level teaspoonfuls instead of 1. It would also be possible to use the yeast, dried or concentrated, an hour or two after dissolving it in water instead of leaving it to stand overnight, but it would not be very strong and you would have to use at least twice the quantity, i.e. 1 dessertspoonful to 1 lb of fondant.

The commercially-made invertase is much more concentrated than yeast water: 1 lb. of fondant will require only 10 drops, from an eye-dropper, of the manufactured invertase to produce a soft centre in 14 days. After adding invertase to fondant it must never be heated above 165°F. or this will kill the invertase. However, the home-made variety must be heated to about 160°F. to ensure that no active yeast cells get into the fondant and subsequently into the chocolates to produce fermentation. When the yeast cells are sterilised they stop producing the strong yeast smell so there is no risk of the chocolates being affected by that.

Preparing Peppermint Fondant for Pouring

Equipment: Starch tray full of cornflour smoothed down and impressed with peppermint cream moulds, a roasting tin half-full of gently simmering water, a casting funnel with its piece of dowel or wooden spoon handle, eye-dropper, a thermometer – the plain glass one used for couverture is best – a board or tray with a sheet of silicone paper, flour sieve.

Ingredients: 1 lb. fondant
10 drops peppermint oil
10 drops invertase or $\frac{1}{4}$ fl. oz. yeast water ($\frac{1}{2}$ dessertspoonful)
pinch citric acid dissolved in very little water
stock syrup.

Method: Break up the fondant and put it in the pan. Put the pan in the gently simmering water and stir with a metal or wooden spoon until it is all melted. Add the invertase or yeast water and citric acid and stir in thoroughly. Allow the fondant to warm up to 160°F. but not over 165°F. At this temperature, the consistency should be similar to double cream. If it is too thick, add a little stock syrup; if it is too thin, either keep the fondant hot until the excess water has evaporated and the fondant thickened or add a little sieved icing sugar. Finally, add the peppermint oil and stir in; this is added at the end to reduce the risk of evaporation. Check the flavour, adding a little more peppermint if you think it necessary.

If you are using a fondant funnel, this should be warmed first to prevent the fondant hardening on contact. The dowel or wooden spoon should be put in to cover the hole and the funnel can be stood upright in a conveniently-shaped jug. Remove the fondant from the hot water, dry the base of the pan and pour all the fondant into the funnel, including the pan scrapings. The funnel is held by the handle and the other hand is used to lift the dowel stopper to allow the fondant to flow into the impressions in the starch tray. Immediately an impression is filled, the stopper is replaced, cutting off the flow. After a little practice, it is possible to deposit fondant very rapidly.

Fondant can be poured straight from the pan, but there are likely to be many stray drips on the starch tray; the flow is difficult to control and the fondant is being poured from a greater height and sometimes buries itself in the cornflour, making irregular shapes. However, small quantities can be poured from a small saucepan which must have a lip, and a tablespoon can be held in the other hand to catch drips.

After about an hour, the fondants should be quite cold and have set hard. Test by picking one out and squeezing it. If it collapses under a little pressure do not attempt to dip them in chocolate, but put them back in the pan, reheat and cast them again. If the test fondant stands up, pick the fondants out with a fork and put them into the flour sieve. Shake gently to remove as much cornflour as possible then give a final dusting with a pastry-brush. The fondants can be arranged on silicone paper and then moved to a warmer room, about 65°F., for dipping. This is necessary because the centres must not be too cold before dipping, but it does soften the fondants and tends to make them slightly moist and sticky on the outside, so they should not be allowed to overlap. After dipping, peppermint creams can be decorated with the four-pronged fork or left plain.

Rose and Violet Creams

Rose and Violet Creams are made in the same way as Peppermint Creams, substituting these flavours for the peppermint. This is one of the occasions when you will have to use chemical rather than natural flavours. Large food stores, such as Selfridges, Harrods and Fortnum and Mason, stock rose and violet flavours. You will have to use a greater quantity of these flavours than of peppermint oil, probably a teaspoonful or more. Also the colour will have to be adjusted with some violet and red food colours, measured with an eye-dropper. The extra liquid may thin the fondant quite a bit, so you will have to be careful. After dipping, these chocolates are decorated with a piece of crystallised rose petal or violet petal which helps enormously to brighten up the look of a box of chocolates.

'Bob' Syrup

It is possible to make a syrup, using the same ingredients as for fondant and cooking it to a similar temperature, then adding a fondant to it, rather like making fudge. The effect is to make the syrup grain in the same way as the fondant, it can then be flavoured and cast in starch. This syrup is known as a 'bob' syrup and helps to economise on the use of fondant, which is quite a consideration if you have to make it yourself. It is also an advantage because the syrup can be cooked to a higher temperature, the final mixture is therefore drier and can take more liquids without becoming too thin for casting.

Equipment: Two 5 in. pans, thermometer, metal spoon, scales, tin of water simmering.

Ingredients: 7 oz. granulated sugar
              1 oz. glucose powder
              2 oz. water
              8 to 12 oz. fondant.

Method: Mix the sugar, glucose and water and bring to the boil in the same way as for fondant. The syrup should be cooked to 250°F., then put on one side until the bubbles have settled. The cold fondant should be added to the syrup, which will be quite hot enough to melt the fondant. The mixture should be well stirred and kept hot in the tin of simmering water. The fondant will grain the syrup and the mixture can be used in the same way as ordinary fondant – after checking the temperature, the yeast water or invertase, acid and flavourings are added, the consistency is adjusted and the mixture deposited in cornflour.

The use of a bob syrup makes it possible to make fondants using yeast water and a fairly liquid concentrate or purée without thinning the fondant too much, so that any of the flavours and colours discussed in the last chapter can be used.

Orange Fondant: 8 oz. bob syrup, 8 oz. fondant, 10 drops of invertase or $\frac{1}{2}$ oz. yeast water (bare tablespoonful), $\frac{1}{4}$ teaspoonful citric acid dissolved in a little water, 5 dessertspoonfuls Sunquick or similar orange concentrate, 1 or 2 teaspoonfuls of grated orange rind.

First make the bob syrup. '8 oz. bob syrup' in these recipes means a bob syrup cooked to 250°F. and made with 7 oz. sugar and 1 oz. glucose. In fact, the weight of such a syrup will be almost 9 oz., including water. Add the rest of the ingredients as described for Peppermint Creams. This recipe will fill about 60 drum-shaped impressions approximately 1 x $\frac{1}{2}$ in.

Lemon Fondant: As for orange fondant, but use lemon concentrate and grated lemon rind.

Raspberry Fondant: As for orange fondant, but using half the citric acid and adding purée made from fresh or frozen raspberries. Adjust the colour with red food colour.

Blackcurrant Fondant: As for orange fondant, but use about half the citric acid. For flavour, try jam melted in a little hot water and sieved, or one of the blackcurrant juice concentrates.

Apricot Fondant: As for orange fondant, using the same amount of citric acid and, for flavour, jam melted in a little hot water and sieved.

A delicious variation for blackcurrant or apricot fondant made with jam is to pour a blob of jam, sieved and thinned with a little water, into the bottom of the moulds before filling up with the flavoured fondant. The jam will set to a jelly and be strong enough to stand dipping in chocolate, thus giving a two-tone centre.

Maraschino Cherries

Maraschino cherries can be made by casting a dome-shaped shell of tempered couverture in a metal or plastic mould. When the shell has set, it is filled with a piece of cherry and a thin mixture of fondant and flavour or liqueur, and a film of tempered couverture is laid on top to seal it and form the base of the chocolate. A similar method is described in the chapter on liqueurs, but it does require the proper moulds and they are not easy to find. There are two alternative methods; casting in starch and pouring into cups.

STARCH-CAST CHERRIES

Ingredients: Bob syrup made with $3\frac{1}{2}$ oz. sugar and $\frac{1}{2}$ oz. glucose and cooked to 250°F.
4 oz. fondant
10 drops invertase or $\frac{1}{2}$ oz. yeast water
pinch citric acid dissolved in a little water
maraschino cherries dried carefully
maraschino liqueur or brandy and the syrup from the cherries
sieved icing sugar.

Method: Impressions are prepared in the starch tray, dome shapes are usual and can be made $\frac{7}{8}$ in. wide and $\frac{7}{8}$ in. deep, from modelling compound. The fondant is heated and mixed in the usual way and the citric acid and invertase added. Thin the fondant down with the liqueur or the brandy and maraschino syrup to give a good flavour. If the fondant becomes too thin, dust in some icing sugar. If yeast water is being used instead of invertase, it will not be possible to use as much flavouring. Quite a lot of invertase is needed because the fondant should become fully liquid as quickly as possible.

Pour a blob of fondant into the impressions and gently press in a half or quarter cherry to prevent it floating to the top.

Fill up with fondant, trying to ensure that the piece of cherry is sealed in. Remove the fondants when hardened and dip in couverture quickly, or the invertase will begin to soften them.

CHERRY CUPS

Ingredients: 8 oz. fondant
maraschino cherries
3 tablespoonfuls of brandy or maraschino liqueur
or 2 tablespoonfuls of brandy and 1 of syrup
from the cherries
10 drops of invertase or ½ oz. yeast water (1
dessertspoonful)
red food colour
pinch of citric acid
12 oz. plain baking chocolate
melted tempered couverture
wax-paper chocolate cases.

Method: Set out the chocolate cases in three or four thicknesses and pour enough couverture in each one to coat the inside fully up to about ⅛ in. from the top. Allow the couverture to harden, then gently peel the paper cases off the chocolate cups and put them in clean cases.

Do not heat the fondant, but mix it with the brandy, liqueur or syrup, the invertase (not the yeast water) and citric acid. Adjust the colour. Yeast water must be heated to 160°F. beforehand to sterilise the yeast cells. This should be done by mixing the yeast water into the fondant and then heating to 160°F.; the other ingredients may be added, but the mixture must be quite cold when it is poured into the chocolate cups. Whether using yeast water or invertase, this mixture is much more liquid than fondant for starch-casting.

Put a piece of cherry, perhaps a third or half a small one, in each chocolate cup and pour in the fondant to not more than two-thirds the depth of the cup. Allow them to stand until the surface skins over slightly.

Meanwhile, melt the baking chocolate and soften it further with a tablespoonful of vegetable fat such as Spry or Trex or vegetable oil, but be careful not to let it overheat. Pour the baking chocolate over the fondant to coat the surface, making sure the edges are properly sealed. A small spoon can be used; start to pour at the edge and work inwards. A better appearance can be achieved by piping the chocolate through an $\frac{1}{8}$ in. plain tube in a forcing bag. The chocolate can be finished with a sprinkling of sugar strands or a few silver balls.

The quantities given in the recipe should fill about 40 cups. They look even more attractive in gold foil cases which can be obtained from Creeds (see p. 149) although they are more expensive than wax-paper or 'glacine' cups.

Other fruits can be treated in this way; for instance, pieces of tinned pineapple or preserved ginger, with suitable colours and flavours.

Opera Cream Fondant Centres

The texture and flavour of fondant can be improved by the addition of condensed milk. This is particularly effective for flavours such as coffee or maple which blend very well with a creamy flavour. There are various ways of adding the condensed milk; it can be cooked with the syrup before it is poured on the slab to be creamed or it can be added to the syrup on the slab as it is being worked. For home-made chocolates, it is perhaps more convenient to add it to the bob syrup at the same time as the fondant. The reason is that this way you only need to make enough for immediate use, Opera Cream fondant does not keep very long.

Ingredients: 8 oz. fondant
           3 oz. full cream sweetened condensed milk
           bob syrup cooked to 250°F. using 7 oz. sugar
           and 1 oz. glucose.

Method: Cook the bob syrup to 250°F. then stir in the fondant and the condensed milk.

Coffee Creams: The above recipe will make 19 oz. fondant. Add 12 drops of invertase or about $\frac{1}{2}$ oz. yeast water ($\frac{3}{4}$ tablespoonful). A pinch of citric acid dissolved in a little water (in hard-water areas) and enough coffee essence or powder to give a good flavour. Adjust the consistency with stock syrup and deposit in the starch tray. After dipping, Coffee Creams can be decorated with imitation coffee beans moulded from coffee-flavoured marzipan thickened with sieved icing sugar.

Maple Creams: As for Coffee Creams but substituting maple flavour for the coffee. You can use pure maple syrup if you can find it. However, in order to incorporate enough maple syrup to give a good flavour without thinning the fondant too much, the amount of condensed milk should be reduced or dispensed with altogether. One ounce of condensed milk is the most you could use in the standard recipe, particularly if the concentrated form of invertase is not available.

Honey Creams: Honey and condensed milk both have a fairly strong flavour and the amount of condensed milk should be reduced to compensate for the thinning effect of the honey. In the standard recipe for Opera Cream Fondant, use only $1\frac{1}{2}$ oz. condensed milk instead of 3 oz., then stir in enough hard honey to flavour before adding 12 drops of invertase or $\frac{3}{4}$ tablespoonful of yeast water, finally depositing the mixture in cornflour. When making the bob syrup, make sure the fondant is well stirred in and has had time to grain the syrup fully, before adding any honey – in fact it is a good idea to leave it on one side for some minutes. Honey, being an invert sugar, will otherwise stop the syrup graining, and leave the mixture too soft to set after being poured, and there is no remedy for this.

Buttercream Fondant

Buttercream fondant is a variation of the Opera Cream fondant.
Vanilla Buttercreams: Cook a bob syrup made with 7 oz. sugar and 1 oz. Glucose to 250°F., allow to cool and stir in 8 oz. fondant, 8 oz. unsalted butter, 10 drops invertase or 1 dessertspoonful yeast water, a pinch of citric acid (hard-water

areas) and 1 to 2 teaspoonfuls of vanilla flavour. Stir well since the butter may take some time to mix, then deposit in the starch tray. This recipe makes a very soft and rich mixture with a strong butter flavour, which is fairly difficult to dip, the high fat content encourages pinholes in the coating. Therefore, buttercreams must be pre-bottomed and until you have gained a considerable amount of experience, it would be wise to make them with less butter, say 2–4 oz. The recipe makes about 90 drums measuring 1 x $\frac{5}{8}$ in.

Brandy Buttercreams: As for vanilla buttercreams but substituting brandy essence.

Praline Buttercreams: Praline is made from almonds or hazelnuts, or both, and sugar. 8 oz. sugar and 6 oz. nuts are put in a pan over heat. Stir slowly with a metal spoon, a wooden one would burn. The sugar will first melt and then colour. Do not allow it to cook quickly and if there is any sign of burning, remove it from the heat. The nuts will gradually start to roast, so take one out and cut it open. When a test nut is fawn colour all through, the mixture is cooked. It can be poured on a greased marble slab or in a greased frying-pan set in cold water. Keep turning the mixture over with a knife to make sure it does not stick. When it is quite cold, break it up and crush the pieces finely on a board with a rolling-pin – hold one end of the rolling-pin down on the board with one hand and lever down with the other. Praline is very hygroscopic and must be kept in a tightly-sealed jar or it will soon become sticky.

For Praline Buttercreams, add 2 tablespoonfuls of praline to the recipe given for Vanilla Buttercreams. The caramelised sugar will dissolve in the centre, but the flavour will remain.

7

Nougat, Marshmallow and Jellies

Nougat

Foam, made from egg or vegetable albumen or from gelatine, is an important ingredient in sweet-making. Added to a hot syrup, its function is to keep it aerated until it cools and sets. The most common forms of this sweet in Britain are nougat and marshmallow, but in America the principle is more widely used in Divinity and Oriental Creams, the latter being a fondant into which stiff egg-whites are worked as the creaming begins. Divinity is a kind of crystalline nougat. An interesting variation sometimes used commercially applies the same principle of aeration as baking powder. A food acid, such as citric, is added to the mix, followed by a quantity of bicarbonate of soda. This creates a fizzy effect and the mixture rises like a sponge cake.

Nougat may be made chewy like a caramel, or short like a candy. The difference is that one is poured as a thick syrup while the other is made to grain, and this is achieved by the quantity of doctoring agent used and the amount of beating – the candy nougat requires less doctor and more beating. However, both forms have to be whipped and there is always the risk that a nougat intended to be chewy will, in fact, candy. This may not happen until some time after the nougat has been made.

Egg albumen, when used to produce foam, gives a better flavour but is more difficult to handle, its foam is less stable and more liable to collapse. It will not foam if there is any grease present, a dash of lemon juice may help, but the bowl and whisk should be kept very clean and it is desirable to soak them in boiling water with a little detergent and then rinse before using them. Better results are achieved if the egg-whites are fresh and almost lukewarm when they are whipped. The syrup, when added to the egg-whites, must be at a sufficiently high temperature to cook them. Once the egg-whites have been added, the nougat cannot be reheated, since egg-whites burn at very low temperatures and, instead of melting, the mixture just browns rapidly.

Gelatine has no flavour, but it foams well and does not collapse so easily. It is not essential that it should be cooked; indeed, if it is heated over 160°F. it can lose its capacity to gel, but this does not affect any of its other characteristics. Nougat made with gelatine can be reheated to a smooth pouring consistency over direct heat without burning. Another significant characteristic is that gelatine makes nougat more chewy and elastic and is sometimes used in caramels for this reason. When used in a candy nougat, gelatine produces a soft, slightly spongy sweet unlike the more brittle egg-white nougat. Gelatine is perhaps preferable for home sweet-making, particularly if you like a chewy nougat, because the result is more predictable.

It is very important in making nougat to cook the syrup to the correct degree of hardness, so that after being whipped into the foam it is firm enough to stand up. Nougat, being aerated, is naturally soft, so the syrup has to be cooked to relatively high temperatures, rarely less than 270°F. As with other forms of sugar confectionery, liquids or thin syrups added to the mixture soften it, and either they should be added to the syrup before the final temperature is reached or the syrup should be cooked harder before the extra ingredients are added. Honey, for instance, is a delightful flavouring agent, essential for Nougat

Montélimar, but too thin to be added after the syrup has been cooked. Therefore, it must be boiled with the syrup, despite the risk of loss of flavour, but in order to minimise this, the honey is added late in the cooking process. A creamy flavour and texture can be achieved by adding a small quantity of condensed milk, but this is added after the syrup has been beaten in, not during the cooking process, so that it does not caramelise; therefore the syrup has to be cooked harder to compensate. Other suitable flavours are chocolate, vanilla, raspberry or lemon, with corresponding colours. But there is no reason why you should not make nougat with less usual flavours, orange, coffee, peppermint, rum or brandy. A multi-layer effect can be obtained by pouring a thin layer of nougat in one flavour, covering it with a different flavour and then, perhaps, adding a third.

Nuts and fruit are often added. Glacé cherries and angelica give flavour and colour, and sultanas and candied peel are occasionally used. Blanched almonds are very popular and pistachio nuts or coconut can be included.

Almonds are blanched by putting the nuts in cold water and bringing it to the boil. Pistachio nuts are put in cold water, brought to the boil and simmered for about 5 minutes. Both are then put under the cold-water tap, and when cold the skins are slipped off by pressing the nut between the fingers. Pistachio nuts are expensive, not easily available and are laborious to skin.

Nougat, like fudge, may be poured out between bars on a wooden or marble slab or into a rectangular tin. If the nougat is to be dipped, these receptacles should be lined with silicone paper; if it is to be wrapped in cellophane, the lining should be of edible rice-paper, which can be obtained from most stationers. After pouring, the nougat is covered with another sheet of rice or silicone paper; if rice-paper is used, the surface of the nougat may have to be moistened slightly with water to make sure it sticks. A board is then placed on top with a weight and it is kept under light pressure for at least 6 hours, by which time it should be quite cold and have set hard. Chewy nougat must be cut with a hot knife and wrapped very quickly after it has set, since it is very hygroscopic and becomes not just sticky, but very runny if left too long. Candy nougat made with gelatine can be cut easily when cold with a sharp knife, but candy nougat made with egg-white should be scored while still warm, since it tends to crumble.

Basic Nougat Recipe

Equipment: 6-in. pan with a lip for better pouring, 5-in. pan, thermometer, metal spoon, pastry-brush, scales, extra-clean heat-resistant glass bowl holding at least $2\frac{1}{2}$ pints, one of $6\frac{1}{2}$ in. diameter should be large enough. An electric mixer is invaluable; nougat could be made by two people using only a hand whisk but the hot syrup must be poured into the foam as it is being beaten. A slab and bars or tin lined with silicone or rice-paper, a board to cover and a weight. If using gelatine, another 6-in. pan will be needed, three-quarters full of hot water.

Ingredients:

      for a candy nougat: 16 oz. granulated sugar
                               4 oz. glucose powder
      for a chewy nougat: 12 oz. granulated sugar
                               8 oz. glucose
          and *either* the white of one large egg
                    ($1\frac{1}{2}$ oz. albumen)
           or $\frac{1}{2}$ oz. gelatine powder (4 level teaspoon-
               fuls – use measuring spoons) soaked in
               1 oz. water ($1\frac{1}{2}$ tablespoonfuls).

Method: Dissolve the sugar and glucose in sufficient water (5 oz. or $\frac{1}{4}$ pint) and bring to the boil, observing the sugar-boiling procedure. Cook the syrup to 270° or 275°F., remove from the heat and dip the base of the pan in water for a moment to check any further cooking. If using egg-whites, these should be whipped to a stiff foam in the heat-resistant bowl. If using gelatine, which should have been soaked in the bowl with the water for at least 10 minutes, put the bowl over the pan of hot water and heat until the gelatine melts, then put the bowl under the mixer. Start beating the stiff egg-whites or the melted gelatine and add the hot syrup in a gradual stream, beating continuously. The syrup must be poured slowly, making sure it is all fully incorporated before more is added. The hot syrup should not be allowed to come into contact with the sides of the bowl or it will set hard and lumpy. As soon as the syrup has all been incorporated, the beater is stopped and the mixture immediately poured on to the paper-lined tray or slab. It must be poured quickly, for if it cools, it cannot be poured, and if using egg-whites, the mixture cannot be reheated. Cover the mixture with another sheet of silicone or rice-paper. For a candy nougat, remove the bowl from the beater as soon as the syrup has been fully incorporated; then beat with a metal spoon until it becomes lumpy and loses its gloss a little. If necessary, put the bowl in the pan of hot water to keep it warm and liquid. Turn the mixture out on the slab and press it down flat with the fingers before covering it with silicone or rice-paper and the weighted board. If using egg-whites, remove the board after half an hour or so while the nougat is still soft, and divide the nougat into bite-sized pieces by pressing a sharp knife into it about $\frac{1}{4}$ in. deep, so as to score it but not cut it through.

This quantity will make a slab of nougat 7 x 10 x $\frac{5}{8}$ in. which will shrink perhaps to $\frac{1}{2}$ in. on cooling. This means that the board to be put over the nougat will have to be 7 x 10 in. The weight put on top of the board can be a 2-lb. bag of sugar. The nougat should be left for 6 hours to harden, and perhaps even longer in warm weather.

Chocolate Nougat: Add 4 oz. of melted plain eating chocolate and stir in immediately after the syrup.

Other Flavours: Flavours such as vanilla or almond are used in relatively small quantities and there is no risk of their softening the nougat appreciably. Nougat, unlike other sweets, cannot be cooked to much higher temperatures to compensate for adding large quantities of thin fluids, since there is very little difference in water content between a syrup cooked to 275°F. and one cooked to 290°F. and there is a risk of the sugar beginning to caramelise above 290°F.

Therefore, if you are using a concentrate, coffee or orange for instance, which is available in a thick syrup, use no more than a tablespoonful. With anything thinner and less concentrated than that, such as rum, it would be safer to use rum flavour.

All flavours or concentrates are beaten into the nougat immediately after the syrup has been incorporated.

Colours: The more usual nougat colours are white, pink or chocolate. Pink is obtained by beating in a few drops of red food colour after the syrup. Brown is usually obtained by adding chocolate, but brown food colour is available if you wish to have the colour without the flavour. Of course, nougat can be coloured with any shade of food colour you wish: orange, green, yellow for lemon or cochineal for raspberry, but the usual rule applies – use the colour appropriate for the flavour.

Nuts and Fruit: Nuts and fruit must always be warmed, so as not to chill the nougat, and added to the mixture after the syrup has been beaten in. The quantities are a matter of personal preference, but the quantities given in the basic nougat recipe would hold up to a 1 lb. of blanched almonds, hazelnuts, glacé cherries or sultanas or a mixture of them. If using only coconut, I would use not more than $\frac{1}{2}$ lb. of desiccated coconut with the basic recipe.

Nougat Montélimar: This delicious and colourful sweet traditionally contains most of the normal additions to nougat such as honey, almonds, glacé cherries and pistachio nuts or angelica. It is made in the same way as the basic nougat recipe, with the addition of the honey for flavour and the nuts and fruit for variety. However, since honey is used in sufficient quantities to give a good flavour and honey is an invert sugar, the amount of glucose powder can be reduced as well as the amount of granulated sugar.

The ingredients I use are:

14 oz. granulated sugar, 2 oz. glucose powder, 4 oz. clear honey, $\frac{1}{2}$ oz. gelatine (4 teaspoonfuls) soaked in 1 oz. water (6 tea-

spoonfuls) and dissolved by heating over a pan of hot water, 8 oz. blanched almonds, 6 oz. glacé cherries, 2 oz. pistachio nuts or angelica.

The sugar and glucose are dissolved in water and cooked to 270°F. The honey is heated in a separate pan and added to the sugar syrup which is then cooked to 275°F. This is immediately poured gradually into the dissolved gelatine, beating fast all the time. Finally, the warmed nuts and fruit are folded in. The almonds and cherries can be cut in half, the pistachio nuts left whole and the angelica chopped into small pieces. The mixture is then poured on to rice or silicone paper, covered with another sheet of paper and a board and kept under pressure for 6 hours or more.

Marshmallows

Marshmallows are not usually found in boxes of chocolates, perhaps because they are normally made so large and out of proportion to other chocolates, and they are also lighter than other centres. Marshmallows are so named because they used to contain marshmallow root and used to be prescribed as a remedy for chest ailments. It is important to make them firm enough to stand up but also spongy and tender, and if they are to be dipped, great care in handling is required. If they are not to be dipped, they are stored in a thick dusting of a mixture of equal parts of cornflour and icing sugar. Marshmallow can be poured in a slab and cut up, or cast into starch moulds like fondant. It can be made from egg-whites, gelatine or agar or a mixture of these, and can be cooked or uncooked. The recipe given here uses gelatine and is not cooked. It is simply an aerated jelly, and must not be heated above 160°F. or the gelatine may lose its strength. It is a very moist marshmallow and will not keep long – even if it gets the chance.

Equipment: 2½-pint heat-resistant bowl, 6-in. pan ¾ full of hot water, electric or hand beater, slab and bars or rectangular tin lined with silicone paper, or oil some greaseproof paper and dust it with cornflour.

Ingredients: ¼ oz. gelatine powder (2 level teaspoonfuls) soaked in 3 fl. oz. water (weigh it) for at least 10 minutes

4 oz. granulated sugar

6 oz. glucose powder

1 teaspoonful

vanilla flavour.

Method: Put the gelatine and water in the bowl to soak for at least 10 minutes. Then put the bowl on the pan and bring the water to the boil. Simmer until the gelatine has entirely dissolved and the liquid is clear. Stir in the sugar, this may take a little time; the hotter the gelatine, the more easily the sugar dissolves, but the gelatine must not exceed 160°F. When the sugar is entirely dissolved, stir in the glucose. This, again, may take some time. If it is obviously not going to dissolve, add the vanilla and, if necessary, add a very little water. When the mixture is quite liquid, beat fast until it reaches a thick foam. It will be necessary to start with a hand-beater even if using an electric one later, otherwise the mixture splashes too much. A few drops of red food colour can be beaten in at this time if pink marshmallow is preferred. Pour the mixture into the prepared tin or slab and allow to cool and set in a cool place, which will take about 4 or 5 hours. If using a tin, it could be put in the refrigerator in summer. This recipe will make a sheet of marshmallow 7 x 8 in. and ⅝ in. thick.

To dip: Melt and temper some couverture and coat the surface of the marshmallow in the tin or on the slab. Allow to set and harden and then overturn the marshmallow and peel off the silicone or greaseproof paper. It will have to be pulled away gently, scraping with a knife at the same time. Cut the marshmallow into convenient pieces by pressing a sharp knife straight into it. The pieces can be dipped in couverture, the chocolate coating giving a firm enough base to lift the marshmallow out of the couverture with a dipping fork. Alternatively, the fingers of the left hand can be coated with couverture, a marshmallow can be put on the fingers and some more couverture poured over until it is thoroughly coated. Then bang the back of the knuckles on the edge of the couverture bowl to settle the couverture and allow the excess to drip off. The marshmallow can then be placed on a silicone sheet or picked off the fingers with a dipping fork and then laid on the sheet. It is important to prevent the warmth of the fingers from overheating the chocolate or it will set with grey streaks. The couverture should feel quite cool on the fingers as you are working it.

Coffee Marshmallow: Add 4 or 5 teaspoonfuls of dry instant coffee to the sugar solution before beating, leave out the vanilla.

Chocolate Marshmallow: Beat in 5 rounded teaspoonfuls of cocoa after the mixture has reached a thick foam.

Jelly

Having used gelatine to set marshmallows, perhaps this is the most suitable place to discuss jellies. Most boxes of chocolates contain only one jelly, a Turkish Delight, but there is no reason why a wide range should not be made using all the flavours discussed in the chapter on fudge and candy. A number of substances can be used to make jellies set, including gum arabic and gum tragacanth, but the more usual ones are pectin, which when acid is added makes a jelly as in jams, but which is, unfortunately, not easily available; starch, which is the usual base for the traditional form of Turkish Delight, but which is fairly difficult to handle unless a specially treated type is used which is available only in the trade; agar, which is made from seaweed and is a great boon to vegetarians but is expensive, and gelatine, which is much cheaper although not so strong as agar but has the advantage of being easily available. Some of these substances can be used in combination, for instance, a starch may be used as a thickener together with gelatine to give the final set. Gelatine makes a slightly rubbery jelly, while agar is short and sets rather cloudy.

For table use, the manufacturers recommend 3 teaspoonfuls of powdered gelatine ($\frac{3}{8}$ oz.) or 2 teaspoonfuls of agar ($\frac{1}{4}$ oz.) to set 1 pint of liquid. But that quantity of gelatine gives too thin a jelly for our purpose, although the agar is just strong enough to stand up to dipping. Of course, the amount of liquid can be reduced to give a stronger jelly, but for chocolate centres something fairly weak is usually more acceptable. In fact, about double the manufacturers' recommended strength of gelatine gives a set strong enough to stand dipping, i.e. 6 teaspoonfuls ($\frac{3}{4}$ oz.) to a pint of liquid. The liquid can include either fruit concentrate or fresh fruit juice. The latter cannot be used in most chocolate centres, but the high water content of juice is not a problem in jellies. If using oranges or lemons, use the grated peel as well.

Jellies can be poured into a rectangular tin or on a slab between bars, both having been lined with silicone paper. When set, the surface can be coated with tempered couverture to pre-bottom it, and then it is turned out and cut into bite-sized pieces with a sharp knife before being dipped. Agar jellies have a moist surface and can be dusted with a little cornflour before dipping. Alternatively, jellies can be poured into cornflour depressions in the starch tray. This is a better idea since it makes a wider choice of shapes available and also because pouring in cornflour dries the surface of agar jellies and gives a thin crust round gelatine jellies which make them easier to handle.

The amount of gelatine or agar required depends on the total bulk of liquid to be set, including sugar. Half a pint of water requires $\frac{3}{8}$ oz. gelatine, but it would require much more gelatine if a pound of sugar were dissolved in the water. It is possible to work out fairly accurately by how much a given amount of sugar increases the total amount of liquid by calculating five-eighths of the weight of the sugar and calling it fluid ounces. For instance, five-eighths of 16 oz. is 10, so 1 lb. of sugar would dissolve to 10 fl. oz. or $\frac{1}{2}$ pint. Therefore, $\frac{1}{2}$ pint of water or water and fruit juice, mixed with 1 lb. of sugar can be regarded as 1 pint of liquid and will require $\frac{3}{4}$ oz. gelatine to set it sufficiently for a chocolate centre. In fact, 1 lb. of sugar to 10 oz. of other liquids would probably be too sweet, and 12 oz. would be enough. This would give a slightly harder set but not enough to be noticeable.

Sugar is necessary, partly as a sweetener and partly to make a syrup thick enough not to be absorbed by the cornflour. A gelatine solution, even when on the point of setting, will run through cornflour very quickly indeed unless it contains a fairly high proportion of sugar. There is not much risk of a mixture crystallising with a proportion of only 12 oz. of sugar to $\frac{1}{2}$ pint of liquid, but even so, the gelatine or agar would prevent it since they are, in effect, doctoring agents.

Orange Jelly

Equipment: Bowl in hot water, starch tray filled with cornflour, smoothed and printed with suitable moulds, small saucepan with a lip.

Ingredients: juice and grated rind of 2 oranges made up to
$\frac{1}{2}$ pint with water
12 oz. granulated sugar
$\frac{3}{4}$ oz. powdered gelatine (6 level teaspoonfuls) or
$\frac{1}{4}$ oz. agar (2 level teaspoonfuls).

Method: For Gelatine: Put the cold liquid in the bowl and add the gelatine. Stir it in and put the bowl in the hot water, the gelatine will dissolve as the liquid warms up. Do not add gelatine to a hot liquid since it may not entirely dissolve. As soon as the mixture has clarified, add the sugar and stir in. Do not allow the mixture to become too hot, it may affect the gelatine. Remove the bowl from the hot water and allow to cool until the jelly begins to thicken, pour it into the cornflour depressions from the small saucepan, using a tablespoon to catch any drips. Put a little cornflour into a fine sieve and dust over the jellies. When they have set, they can be lifted out with a fork, tossed in a flour sieve like fondant centres and brushed before they are dipped in tempered couverture.

For Agar: Put the liquid in the saucepan and stir in the agar. It will have to be brought almost to the boil before the agar dissolves. If it does boil, the set is not affected. Stir in the sugar, reheating if necessary, then allow the mixture to cool before pouring it into the cornflour depressions. As with gelatine jellies, dust over with cornflour and allow to set before dipping. The disadvantage of agar is that since it must be brought to such a high temperature, some flavour may be lost.

From this basic Orange Jelly recipe it is possible to make any other flavour simply by exchanging the orange juice for another fruit juice such as grapefruit or raspberry, for instance. Bottled apple juice can be used or even cider. Strawberries can be puréed and other fruits can be stewed and puréed, and brandy, rum or liqueurs can be added. The important thing is to use not more than $\frac{1}{2}$ pint of liquid, 12–16 oz. of sugar, and $\frac{3}{4}$ oz. gelatine or $\frac{1}{4}$ oz. agar. The one exception is pineapple, either tinned or fresh, which contains an enzyme able to stop gelatine setting. However, this can be sterilised by bringing the pineapple and juice to the boil for a few moments.

Turkish Delight is a little different. It should be made from a starch such as cornflour or arrowroot, which is mixed with enough cold water to wet it thoroughly, then a quantity of water equal to at least eight times the weight of starch is brought to the boil and enough sugar to sweeten is added, followed by the wetted starch. The mixture is stirred until it thickens and becomes almost clear, which indicates that the starch has cooked or 'gelatinised'. Usually arrowroot becomes quite clear, but cornflour remains a little cloudy, though sugar helps to clarify it as it does when added to jam. In fact, the tiny starch grains absorb the water and if a lower proportion of water is used, the starch is unable to gelatinise, the mixture then remains very cloudy and has an unpleasant taste. However, when it has cooked properly, the mixture is still too thin to set into a jelly and it has to be kept boiling on a low light to evaporate a high proportion of its water content.

Starch does not burn readily like a liquid thickened with flour but stirring is needed to prevent it from forming hard lumps. It is ready when it is reduced to about a quarter of its original bulk and when it begins to turn stringy and slightly dry to the touch. It is then flavoured and poured into trays greased and dusted with either cornflour or a mixture of equal parts of cornflour and icing sugar. The problem is that when normal starches have been cooked to the right consistency they become too thick to pour. Professional chocolatiers are able to solve this by using specially treated starches which are quite thin even after prolonged boiling, and produce the same jelly-like consistency as ordinary starches when cool.

Home chocolatiers must spoon the jelly out of the pan in lumps, drop it into the receptacle, dust cornflour over the top and press the mixture to shape with the fingers. It is then allowed to cool and set. If it is intended to dip the jelly, the loose cornflour is dusted off with a brush and the surface can be coated with tempered couverture in the same way as for marshmallow. When this has hardened, the jelly is turned out, chocolate-side down, any loose cornflour is dusted off and it is cut into bite-sized pieces. The pieces can then be fork-dipped, the chocolate base being sufficiently firm to allow the jellies to be lifted out of the couverture bowl.

The usual flavours for Turkish Delight are rose, which is tinted red, and lemon, which is left colourless. The rose flavour is more usual in chocolate centres.

Turkish Delight

Equipment: Scales, ½-pint cup or small bowl, 6-in. pan, asbestos mat, small rectangular tin or slab and bars greased and dusted with cornflour or lined with silicone paper.

Ingredients: 6 oz. granulated sugar
                1 oz. cornflour or arrowroot (8 rounded teaspoonfuls)
                ½ pint water
                red food colour and rose flavour, or lemon flavour and lemon juice, or citric acid.

Method: Put the starch into the bowl and add enough water to mix. Put the rest of the water in the pan, preferably a thick one, add the sugar and dissolve it over heat. Pour in the starch and reheat, stirring to prevent lumps until it has clarified and much of the cloudiness has disappeared. Then put the pan on the asbestos mat over a low light and allow the mixture to simmer slowly, stirring occasionally until it becomes quite thick and instead of dropping off the spoon it hangs in strands. It can be tested for thickness by dropping a blob on a cold plate. Allow the mixture to cool a little, then stir in the flavours and transfer to the tin or slab. Dust over with cornflour, or a mixture of equal parts of cornflour and icing sugar, and press into shape. This recipe will make a slab about 5 x 5 in. and about $\frac{5}{8}$ in. thick. When the jelly has cooled, it can be turned out, dusted, cut up and dipped.

8

Marzipan

There are two methods of making marzipan. In one, the 'German' method, ground almonds and sugar are mixed together and cooked; in the other, sugar and water are cooked to about 240°F. and poured on to ground almonds. There is no advantage in either method, since it is quite easy to buy marzipan which has good flavour and excellent consistency. It should not be confused with almond paste which is made from equal amounts of ground almonds and sometimes a few hazelnuts, and icing sugar, moistened with a little water or eggwhite.

Marzipan can be dipped in chocolate or in fondant which is then crystallised. Alternatively, marzipan can be given a variety of different colours and flavours which are then combined in layers like Battenburg Cake, cut into slices and crystallised. The purpose of crystallising is to keep sweets moist and to prevent drying out. A few pieces of crystallised marzipan or fondant give colour to a box of chocolates – therefore the next chapter gives instructions on crystallising.

Marzipan bought from the shops is too soft and tends to crumble. It can be made to hold together by adding sieved icing sugar and it is capable of holding up to equal its own weight of icing sugar. This is mixed to the consistency of clay; it can be rolled out like pastry or cut into pieces which are then pressed into shape.

CHOCOLATE-DIPPED MARZIPAN

Green is a characteristic colour for marzipan and is added by breaking up the raw marzipan, sprinkling on a few drops of green food colour and moulding it into the marzipan until it is evenly distributed. A few drops of almond essence can be added to strengthen the flavour. It is easier to colour marzipan before adding icing sugar since it is not so stiff at that point. Flatten out the marzipan roughly on a board, dust thickly with sieved icing sugar, fold the marzipan over to seal the icing sugar inside, flatten again, dust with icing sugar, fold, flatten and so on until the marzipan has attained the consistency you prefer. It should feel fairly dry and not sticky.

Green marzipan can be used to stuff dates – the stone is removed and the cavity filled with a piece of marzipan. It can be mixed with chopped, preserved ginger, taking care that the pieces of ginger are properly dried before being folded into the marzipan. When thoroughly blended, pieces of the mixture can be dusted with icing sugar, then allowed to dry a little before being dipped. These chocolates can be decorated with a little piece of crystallised ginger. Chopped walnuts can also be folded into marzipan in the same way as ginger, pieces can be pulled off, moulded to shape and allowed to crust before being dipped and decorated with a small piece of walnut.

A glacé cherry can be wrapped up in a piece of marzipan coloured pink with a few drops of red food colour. With care, it is possible to dry a maraschino cherry sufficiently to use it in the same way in this case the marzipan can be flavoured with cherry brandy as well as being coloured.

For chocolate marzipan, fold in sieved cocoa, followed by icing sugar until the mixture reaches the correct consistency. A piece of green marzipan and a piece of chocolate marzipan can be rolled out with a rolling-pin to about 5/16 in. thick, dusting with sieved icing sugar as necessary. Stamp out rounds with a 1-in. plain cutter and stick a green disc on top of a brown one with a dab of water or egg-white. These can be dipped and decorated with little pieces of brown and green marzipan rolled very thinly and cut into tiny triangles or diamonds.

Many other flavours can be added to marzipan which blend well with its natural almond taste. Among the liqueurs, Kirsch is particularly suitable. The usual fruit concentrates can be used – orange, lemon or grapefruit – together with suitable adjustment of colour. When using liquids it is, as usual, important not to include so much that the mixture is too soft to stand up to dipping.

Marzipan flavoured with liqueurs or concentrates can be rolled out, dusted with sieved icing sugar as necessary, and cut into simple squares or diamonds. Allow to stand a little time to crust. It will probably be essential to pre-bottom them before dipping; alternatively, the surface of the whole sheet of marzipan can be coated with couverture before being turned over, chocolate-side down, and then cut into pieces for dipping.

Chocolate logs: These can be made with vanilla truffle (see the chapter on Truffles) and green marzipan. The mixture is delicious and colourful, since it is only partly dipped in couverture. The truffle mixture is rolled out into a rope of barely $\frac{3}{4}$ in. diameter, using sieved cocoa as necessary. A piece of green marzipan is then rolled out with a rolling-pin to about $\frac{1}{8}$ in. thick, $3\frac{1}{2}$ in. wide and as long as the truffle rope. With a small sharp knife, cut along the long edge of the marzipan so that, instead of its being cut off square, it is undercut at an angle of about 45° or so. Moisten the surface of the marzipan with a little water or egg-white, lay the truffle rope on top and roll it up in the marzipan, lifting the undercut edge first and rolling towards the other edge. Try to roll it fairly tightly so as not to trap any air bubbles inside. When the truffle is completely covered, there will be a little flap of marzipan covering the edge you cut off at an angle, this is trimmed off and the join pressed together to give an even marzipan coating.

The roll should be put in a cold place, such as the refrigerator, for a few hours to allow the truffle mixture to set and the marzipan to crust, otherwise it is very difficult to cut. When the

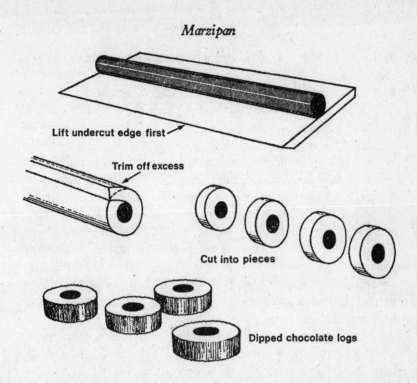

Marzipan

Lift undercut edge first

Trim off excess

Cut into pieces

Dipped chocolate logs

roll has hardened, it is cut into pieces about $\frac{1}{2}$ in. thick with a sharp knife; these can be cut straight or at an angle. The pieces are dipped in tempered couverture but leaving one cut side visible. You will need a dipping fork with the prongs at an angle to the handle; it is very difficult to coat the bottom and the sides without allowing some couverture to wash on to the surface. An ordinary household fork might serve so long as it is not too cold.

CRYSTALLISED MARZIPAN

The use of marzipan as a centre for a fondant coating is dealt with later under Bon-Bons and so is the process of crystallising. Marzipan can be eaten without being crystallised, but it does dry and harden quite quickly and it is then much less pleasant to eat. Although the process requires some additional equipment, it is an interesting one. The pieces of marzipan are put into a tray, covered with a sugar syrup and left to stand until they are completely sealed with a coating of fine sugar crystals. The pieces are then lifted out and put in a warm place to dry.

There are various shapes, designs and colours of marzipan which can be made up into pieces for crystallising. The marzipan is flavoured and coloured to match, and up to four colours can be used in one piece. Green, chocolate, pink and lemon or natural marzipan are commonly used. The pieces are usually cut not more than 1 in. square or 1 in. diameter and ½ in. thick, and laid with the cut side up.

Three-colour Roll: Take three pieces of marzipan suitably coloured and flavoured, say green, chocolate and pink, with enough icing sugar folded in to give a firm consistency. Roll the pink marzipan to a rope shape a little thicker than a pencil. Roll out the chocolate marzipan to a rectangle, at least 1½ in. wide and a good ⅛ in. thick. Take the sheet of chocolate marzipan and lay a ruler along one long edge and, with a sharp knife, trim the edge, not so that it is cut off square, but cut under the ruler at an angle of about 45° in the same way as with the chocolate logs. Do the same with the green marzipan but roll it to 3¼ in. wide. Moisten both sheets of marzipan with a little water or egg-white, lay the pink marzipan on the chocolate and

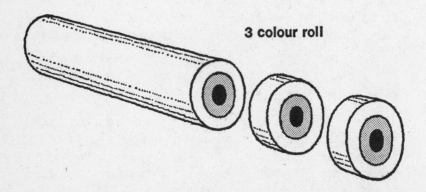

3 colour roll

roll it up, lifting the angled edge and rolling towards the other edge. Trim off the excess marzipan and roll up in the green marzipan in the same way. Let the roll stand in a cool place for a few hours until it has dried sufficiently for you to cut it without pressing it out of shape. Cut $\frac{1}{2}$-in. pieces off the roll with a sharp knife.

Three-colour Square: Roll out a piece of chocolate marzipan and a piece of green about $\frac{1}{4}$ in. thick and cut into strips $\frac{1}{4}$ in. wide. There should be four chocolate strips and five green, all of equal length. Roll out a piece of uncoloured marzipan $4\frac{1}{2}$ in. wide, $\frac{1}{8}$ in. thick or less and the same length as the strips. Arrange the strips in layers so that the bottom layer has a green strip on either side of a chocolate strip. Moisten with a little water or egg-white and cover with two chocolate strips and one green, the green one being in the middle. Moisten, and add the third layer of two green strips with the chocolate one in the middle. The nine strips are now stuck together in a long bar.

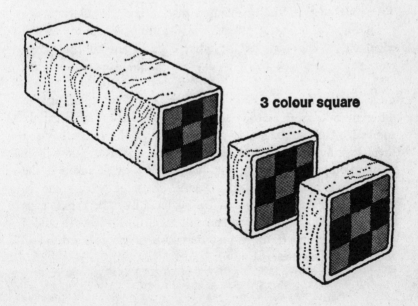

3 colour square

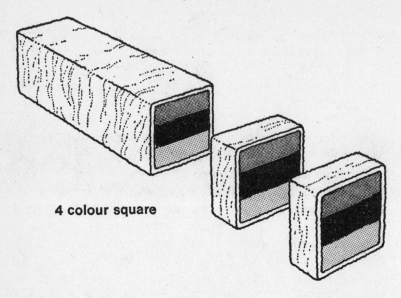

4 colour square

Trim one edge of the uncoloured marzipan at an angle as described above, lay the strips on it and roll up, lifting the angled edge and rolling towards the other edge. Trim off the excess marzipan. Allow the block to dry out on the surface, then cut off $\frac{1}{2}$-in. pieces.

Four-colour Square: Roll out three strips of marzipan in different colours, $\frac{3}{4}$ in wide and $\frac{1}{4}$ in. thick and of equal length, squared off at the edges. Lay one on top of the other, sticking them together with dabs of water or egg-white. Roll out a piece of uncoloured marzipan $4\frac{1}{2}$ in. wide and $\frac{1}{8}$ in. thick and the same length as the three strips. Trim one edge at an angle, as described earlier, and moisten the surface. Lay the three strips on the uncoloured marzipan and roll them up, lifting the angled edge first. Trim off the excess marzipan, allow to harden and then cut off $\frac{1}{2}$-in. pieces.

9

Bon-bons

Bon-bons or 'Fourres' are not chocolates but are not out of place in this book because, like crystallised marzipan, they give colour and variety to a box of chocolates. They are basically a centre, usually made of fondant or marzipan, dipped in fondant and crystallised. Therefore, we can look first at the centres and how they are made, secondly at the way the centres are dipped and lastly how the coated bon-bons are crystallised.

BON-BON CENTRES

Marzipan for centres must be firm enough to be moulded, and can be flavoured and coloured in the way described in the last chapter. Flavours can include orange, lemon or grapefruit concentrates and purées such as raspberry or blackcurrant. Enough icing sugar is worked in to give a fairly firm consistency. Small pieces of the mixture are moulded to shape and should not be too large; bon-bons are usually drum or dome-shaped and a maximum size would be $\frac{7}{8}$ in. diameter by $\frac{1}{2}$ in. deep for a drum, or $\frac{7}{8}$ x $\frac{3}{4}$ in. for the dome. The pieces are then left a few hours to crust before being dipped.

Fondant centres are cast in cornflour in exactly the same way as fondants for dipping in couverture. You will need to make suitable moulds for them. The same flavours can be used although orange, lemon, raspberry, coffee and peppermint are most usual. After casting, the centres are removed from the cornflour, sieved and dusted and can be set out on silicone paper to await dipping. Invertase is not used in bon-bons because it liquidizes not only the centre, but also the fondant in which it is dipped and even the fine coating of crystals, so that the bon-bon eventually collapses.

Fondant Dipping

Some chocolatiers recommend a special fondant for coating bon-bons, using an acid or acid substance rather than glucose as the doctor, but this is not essential. An ordinary fondant is just as successful.

Equipment: A double-boiler, or even better, a saucepan, wider at the rim than the base which will fit about half-way inside a straight-sided pan. A tray or board, covered with a sheet of silicone paper is needed to receive the coated fondants. A ring dipping fork and a glass thermometer of the sort used for testing couverture will be needed.

Ingredients: At least 1 lb. fondant, a supply of stock syrup (2 tablespoonfuls granulated sugar dissolved in 1 tablespoonful of water). Appropriate food colours should be available but not flavours since it is not usual to flavour bon-bon coatings. The colour of the coating can be the same as the colour of the centre, but that is a matter of personal preference.

Method: Put water in the base of the double-boiler or the straight-sided pan so there is enough to reach the upper pan. Bring the water to the boil and put the fondant in the upper pan to soften. Add up to a tablespoonful of stock syrup and food colour and stir in. When the fondant has softened to a liquid, the colour should be corrected and the fondant stirred well. Take the temperature of the fondant – it should be about 160°F. and not less than 150°F. At this temperature, it should have the consistency of single cream; if it is too thick, add a little more stock syrup, if it is too thin, just keep stirring until enough water has evaporated to thicken it. Try not to thin it too much since this is a long process. It will be necessary to keep the water under the pan very hot, if not boiling, particularly when you are dipping, since the cold fondants cool the mixture.

The centres and the empty board will have to be arranged close to the pan. The board covered with silicone paper could be placed next to the cooker. There is no need to worry about the temperature of the room in which you are working, nor the temperature of the centres or the dipping-fork as you do when dipping in chocolate. Nor is there any need to pre-bottom the centres, since the fondant coating is much thicker than chocolate, nor to worry about air-bubbles. Most important, the fondant is not tempered but it does have to be stirred constantly, not just to stop a crust forming, but stirring seems to keep it much more fluid.

Drop a centre into the fondant, submerge it and lift it out with the ring-fork. Transfer it to the silicone paper and quickly invert the fork allowing the fondant to drop on to the paper. Touch the the top of the fondant with the fork and pick up a blob of still-liquid fondant, then lift the fork and make a trail in the same way as for chocolates. This little flourish is not easy and you will have to dip hundreds before you can achieve a really professional finish, but this is not necessary for home-made products. However, the fondant must be at the correct consistency, it should be kept well-stirred, and the centres must be dropped and marked very quickly, before the fondant sets. If you have those three things right, the process will be much easier. As you become more experienced, you will be able to produce the correct consistency without the use of a thermometer. After an hour or two, the bon-bons are ready to be eaten, or they can be crystallised, which prevents them from drying out.

EQUIPMENT FOR CRYSTALLISING

The object of crystallising is to coat the fondant or marzipan pieces with a fine covering of sugar crystals, sealing them so that the centres do not dry out and harden and also giving them an attractive appearance.

The pieces are submerged in a solution of granulated sugar and water in which the concentration of sugar must be absolutely accurate. This sugar syrup is made by dissolving granulated sugar in sufficient water and bringing it to the boil. There must be no stirring or agitation which might encourage premature graining, since no doctoring agents are added to restrain grain. When the syrup has cooled to room temperature, the pieces to be crystallised are set in a tray and the syrup is poured over. They are left in the syrup until they have been adequately coated with crystals. The action of pouring the syrup over the pieces helps to start the graining process.

Crystals will begin to form on the pieces and also on the sides and bottom of the tray. When the crystals are large enough, the pieces are taken out, placed on a wire grid and allowed to drain. The syrup remaining on the pieces turns into crystals and, in time, the surface of each piece becomes quite dry and completely covered with fine, even crystals, almost as though it had been dusted with sugar.

The degree of concentration of the syrup is quite critical. If the syrup is too weak the fondants will melt or the marzipan go soggy. If it is too thick and has too much sugar, the pieces will have a glassy or lumpy finish. The syrup is tested with an instrument called a hydrometer.

As we have seen in earlier chapters, a thermometer is very accurate in indicating sugar strength in a boiling syrup, but it is more accurate aboove 235°F. than below, and at about 222°F. it is just not accurate enough. Half a degree of temperature can make an enormous difference to the strength of a syrup solution, and this is shown more clearly on a hydrometer than a thermometer.

Hydrometers are quite cheap and are rather like a fishing float but made of glass and weighted at the bottom. The upper part has a numbered scale, and the hydrometer is floated in the liquid to be tested and the number at the surface of the liquid gives its strength. If the liquid is very thin, the hydrometer will sink farther than if it is thicker. In the case of a sugar solution, the more sugar that is dissolved in the water, the thicker will be the syrup, the less will the hydrometer sink and the higher will be the reading. There are different kinds of hydrometers for different purposes. For sugar work, the usual hydrometer is the Baumé hydrometer measuring from 0° to 50°. On this instrument, pure water registers 0°, and 50° indicates a very thick syrup. These degrees are written 0°Bé and 50°Bé, for Baumé, to distinguish them from readings of other kinds of hydrometers.

A hydrometer should be checked from time to time since, like a thermometer, it may not always be quite accurate. The way to do this is to float the hydrometer in ordinary tap water when the water temperature is that marked on the hydrometer, usually 60°F. It should give a reading of 0° precisely. If it doesn't, an allowance will have to be made with any other readings you take.

Since the hydrometer measures how thick a syrup is, and since a sugar syrup is thinner when it is hot, the hydrometer gives a lower reading when a syrup is hot. A syrup which gives a reading of 33°Bé at boiling-point will give a reading of about $37\frac{1}{2}°$ when the syrup has cooled to a normal room temperature of about 65°F. Because the readings vary with the temperature, hydrometer readings for sugar boiling are usually given at boiling-point. Therefore, if a recipe specifies a syrup concentrated to 34°Bé, it means that the hydrometer registers 34 when the syrup is at boiling-point. The reason for this is that professional sugar boilers work with large vats of syrup and keep a hydrometer floating in the syrup as it is boiling, until it registers the correct concentration. It would be impracticable in commercial work to take a sample, cool it to a standard temperature and then measure it, since by this time the syrup would have boiled away and become much thicker.

Unfortunately, the home sweetmaker does not cook sugar in

such large quantities. A quantity of syrup sufficient to float a hydrometer in is quite a lot of syrup. Moreover, the professionals use brass hydrometers which are less liable to damage. Therefore, an extra piece of equipment is needed: a glass cylinder or vase, in which the hydrometer can be floated after the syrup has been poured in. Of course, both cylinder and hydrometer must be quite warm before being exposed to the hot syrup or they would crack. Also, this process inevitably means the syrup cools down a little and therefore is slightly thicker than it would be at boiling-point. But it should be possible to keep the syrup sufficiently hot to take a reading at a temperature of 205–210°F. Since the boiling-point of the sugar syrup we will use is about 222–224°F., a small allowance can be made, but for most purposes a reading taken at these slightly lower temperatures is accurate enough.

Hydrometers and cylinders can be purchased from manufacturers of scientific instruments such as Messrs Gallenkamp & Co. Ltd., 6 Christopher St., London E.C.2. A Baumé hydrometer reading 0° to 50° must be specified, and a glass cylinder $9\frac{1}{2}$–10 in. deep and $1\frac{1}{2}$ in. diameter. A cylinder with a larger diameter could be used but it requires more syrup to fill it.

In fact, a much more convenient instrument is available which measures the proportion of solids in a liquid and only requires a blob of the liquid to test. This is called a refractometer, but it is unfortunately very expensive. However, with this instrument there is no need to worry about syrup temperatures and tests can be carried out instantly.

The other equipment needed for crystallising is a tray and a wire grid. Fondant pieces to be crystallised are placed on the rack which is then put inside the tray, and the crystallising syrup is poured over. Special crystallising pans and wires are available, or they can be made to order by G. F. & H. J. Mathews (see p. 149). A useful size is 12 x 8 x 2 in. deep, but small quantities can be crystallised quite easily in the grill pan on your cooker, which also has a wire rack to fit. It would, in

Bon-bons

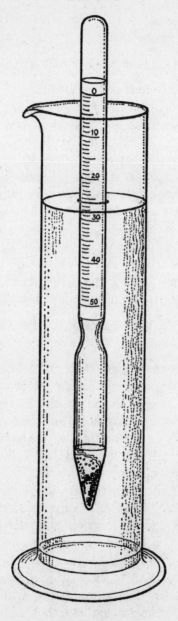

Baumé Hydrometer

any case, be a good idea to start with one of these until you become more experienced.

The first step is to prepare the crystallising syrup. It is necessary to know exactly how much syrup you require, and the best way to find out is to put the wire grid in the tray and fill it up with water to the point at which the centres would just be covered. Then pour the water out and measure it. In fact, you will not need as large a quantity as that since the centres will occupy some space and make the syrup level higher, but it is disastrous to have too little syrup. To make 1 pint of syrup you will need about 1 lb. 2 oz. of sugar.

Equipment: A pan large enough to take the required quantity of syrup with a lip for easy pouring, 5-in. pan, thermometer, scales, pastry-brush, hydrometer and cylinder put to warm, disc of greaseproof paper cut out to fit just inside the syrup pan.

Ingredients: 1 lb. 2 oz. granulated sugar and 5 oz. water for each pint of syrup required.

Method: The 5-in. pan is filled with cold water, the thermometer is put in and the pan is brought to the boil. Check the thermometer reading, it should be 212°F. Observing the sugar boiling precautions very carefully, bring the sugar and water to the boil, washing down the sides of the pan and making sure all the sugar crystals are fully dissolved before the syrup boils. When the syrup boils, put in the thermometer and you will find it soon reads 220°F. Boil fairly quickly, moving the thermometer about gently to ensure a correct reading. When the temperature reaches 222°F., remove from the heat and put the thermometer back in the hot water in the small pan.

The glass cylinder should be quite warm by now, and the hot syrup can be poured in to three-quarters full. Then put in the warmed hydrometer. The safest way is to dip the hydrometer into the syrup for an instant, and then withdraw it, then dip and withdraw and finally put it back slowly. This is to make sure the glass is warm enough not to crack in the hot syrup. The temperature of the syrup in the cylinder should be about 205–210°F. and the hydrometer should read 33½°. This means that the syrup is concentrated to 33° at boiling-point, the extra ½° is to compensate for the slightly lower temperature. If the temperature were lower, say 190°F., the hydrometer reading would be 34°. In fact, the syrup thickens by about 1°Bé for each drop in syrup temperature of 35–40°F., so the same syrup at a temperature of 150°F. would give a reading of 35°Bé on the hydrometer.

Crystallising syrups are normally concentrated to 33–36°Bé at boiling-point, depending upon the kind of finish required. A 33°Bé syrup gives a fine crystal suitable for fondants and marzipan pieces, and a 36°Bé syrup gives a much coarser crystal such as is found on jellies. Therefore, if we aim at a 33°Bé syrup and it is, in fact, a little thicker, say 34°Bé, it will still be quite safe to use.

If the syrup is only 32°Bé, it is too thin and should be poured back into the pan and cooked a little longer. If, however, the syrup reads 34°Bé or more at 205–210°F., it is a little too thick. In this case, add a little boiling water to the syrup in the cylinder and stir gently until you get the correct reading. This will give you some indication of how much water you need to add to the syrup in the pan to give the correct degree of concentration. Return the syrup to the pan, bring to the boil and test again.

When the syrup has reached the correct degree, remove the pan to a cool, heatproof surface where it can remain completely undisturbed for 5 or 6 hours until it has cooled. Take the disc of greaseproof paper moisten it and lay it on the surface of the syrup. This will keep out dust particles and also prevent the syrup forming a crust over its surface. The syrup is ready for use when it feels cool to the touch and the temperature is 90°F. or less.

If, when the syrup has cooled, you think it may not be of the correct concentration, do not reheat it, for that would concentrate it further. It can be tested with the hydrometer by pouring a sample into the cylinder very carefully so as not to encourage grain, then take a reading with the hydrometer. At a normal room temperature of 65°F., a syrup concentrated to 33°Bé at boiling point will have thickened to 37½°Bé. A 36°Bé syrup will have cooled to 40½°Bé. If the syrup is thicker than it should be, a little water or a thin solution of sugar and water can be added, stirring gently. However, water does not mix easily with a cold syrup and a lot of stirring encourages grain, so it is preferable to get it right while the syrup is hot.

The next step is to prepare the pieces to be crystallised. The crystallising pan and grid are required and should be, at least, fairly dry. Another grid or rack will be needed on which the pieces can be put to drain. The grid is made so that, placed in the pan one way, it is close to the base of the pan, but put in the other way up it is nearer to the top of the pan. Sometimes, two grids are used at the same time, one in the low position and one high. The main function of the higher one in this case is to attract the surface crust and enable it to be removed easily. However, this is not essential, but the grid should be used in the low position when crystallising fondants, since they sink and have to be kept just off the bottom to ensure that the undersides are crystallised. Marzipan pieces, however, float and have to be kept submerged, so the grid is put in the high position on top of the pieces.

After the pieces have been arranged in the crystallising pan, fondants on top of the grid or marzipan underneath, the pan is set in a convenient place where it will not be disturbed. Then the greaseproof sheet is removed from the surface of the crystallising syrup and the syrup is poured gently into the crystallising pan until the pieces are nicely submerged. Some rearrangement of the pieces may be necessary since they should not touch each other or the sides of the pan or they will stick.

The pieces should be allowed to remain in the syrup for about 12 hours. At this point, a piece can be taken out to see whether it has a good coating of crystals; if not, it can be put back and left for another few hours. A thicker syrup, besides producing a coarser crystal, also crystallises more quickly, and a 36°Bé syrup may only take about 6 hours. The pieces should now be removed from the syrup and placed on the other rack or grid to drain. After 2 hours or so, they can be moved a little to prevent sticking to the grid. After they have drained, the pieces can be put in a warm place to dry. This can take some hours and should not be hurried. They can then be stored at a cool temperature.

The crystallising syrup could be reboiled and used again after sufficient water has been added to ensure the crystals have properly dissolved. However, it should not be used a third time. The action of boiling sugar creates invert sugar, invert sugar does not crystallise, and therefore syrup used more than twice becomes unpredictable. The syrup need not be wasted however, it can be used as stock syrup or to make fondant by adding an ounce or two of glucose powder to each pound of syrup. Too much boiling also discolours sugar and makes it turn brown, it is then unsuitable for making into fondant for white centres such as peppermints, but can be used for tinted centres.

10

Liqueurs

The Maraschino Cherry chocolates and the Cherry Cups described on (p. 99) are sometimes referred to as liqueurs. In the former, fondant flavoured with maraschino or brandy and treated with invertase is cast in starch moulds, and after being dipped, the fondant liquefies through the action of the invertase. Cherry Cups are basically a chocolate mould filled with fondant thinned with a liqueur or a spirit such as brandy, the top being sealed with a softened chocolate mixture.

Another form of liqueur is made by casting a shell of couverture in metal or plastic moulds which can be shaped like a bottle. There are several different types of these moulds but the principle of using them is broadly the same. They are usually made as one tray in which there are about ten impressions. They are very expensive and it is a nuisance if you only have one or two to work with, since you have to wait until one set of shells is ready before being able to cast a second batch. During this time, your bowl of tempered couverture may have set as well.

The moulds are filled with tempered couverture. Sometimes couverture is brushed on the insides of the moulds before the chocolate is poured, to reduce the risk of air-bubbles. The moulds are then tapped to encourage any air-bubbles to rise to the surface. If using clear plastic or perspex moulds, you can see air-bubbles through the plastic. After a few moments, the moulds are inverted and the excess couverture allowed to drain out. A plastic spatula can be used to wipe off the liquid couverture, encouraging it, if necessary, with a few taps. The mould should then be laid flat, still inverted, on silicone or wax paper. As the small quantity of excess couverture remaining continues to drain from the mould, it builds up a small lip round the edge of each bottle shape which is an enormous aid to sealing the shells.

The moulds are now allowed to cool until the couverture has set but has not yet hardened. The paper can be peeled off and spirits or liqueurs poured into the shells. Do not fill them more than two-thirds full. Cover a piece of aluminium kitchen foil with a patch of couverture to a depth of about $\frac{1}{8}$ in. and the same size as the mould, making sure there are no air-bubbles. Invert the foil, couverture side down, over the mould and press down. Run your finger round the edge of each mould to ensure that there is a good join and that each shell is sealed off from the couverture between each mould. The mould should be put in a cool place to allow the couverture to set quite hard. Then the aluminium foil is peeled off – foil is used because it gives a better gloss than silicone or wax paper – and the liqueurs are released from the moulds. As the chocolate cools, it also contracts and pulls away fractionally from the sides of the mould, thus the liqueurs actually release themselves. Plastic moulds can be inverted and bent slightly, and if given a sharp tap with the handle of a knife the liqueurs should fall out without difficulty. If they do not, it is probably because they have not hardened enough and therefore have not shrunk sufficiently.

The edge of the liqueurs can be pared smooth with a sharp knife, but it is a good idea to handle the liqueurs with a soft cloth to prevent the fingers melting the surface of the chocolate and spoiling the gloss. Check to make sure there are no leaks – any holes can be patched with a little tempered couverture.

I think it is essential to practise making complete shells without putting any liquid in. It is a tricky operation for which quite a lot of experience is needed. The empty shells can, of course, be melted down again and put back in with your couverture, so there is no waste. If any liquid touches the edges of the shells before the couverture-coated foil is laid over them, it will prevent a good seal and the liquid will leak. For this reason, it is absolutely essential to pour the liquid in with very great care and to make sure the mould is kept perfectly flat and never allowed to tip up. If a pure liqueur or spirit is found to be too strong, it can be diluted with a little water.

Moulds suitable for liqueurs are not easy to obtain, but Creeds (see p. 149) stock plastic ones in two different shapes.

The other form of liqueur is made by preparing a sugar syrup, adding spirit or liqueur and pouring it into cornflour depressions. After standing for some hours, a fragile shell will form enabling the liqueur to be picked out of the cornflour and coated with couverture. Just as truffles are the most delightful chocolates to eat, these liqueurs are, for me at least, the most exciting to make.

The sugar syrup is made from granulated sugar and water only. No doctoring agent is used. The sugar is dissolved in as little water as possible in order to keep the boiling time short – lengthy boiling, as pointed out in the last chapter, has the same effect as a doctor, it inhibits grain and that is to be avoided. The usual precautions for sugar-boiling should be observed: ensuring all sugar crystals are dissolved before the syrup comes to the boil, washing down the sides of the pan, and after the syrup has reached boiling-point there must be no further stirring but the lid can be put on for a few moments.

The syrup is usually cooked to a concentration of 38°Bé which is reached at a temperature of about 227°F. This concentration is quite critical and must be checked with a hydrometer in the same way as the crystallising syrup for bon-bons – the boiling syrup is poured into a glass cylinder and the hydrometer added, the cylinder and hydrometer having both been heated to prevent cracking. The syrup in the cylinder will have cooled to less than boiling-point, which is the temperature at which hydrometer readings should be taken, therefore allowance will have to be made for this, since the syrup will slightly thicken as it cools. If the syrup is really boiling when poured into the cylinder, the temperature should still be about 205–210°F. The reading at this temperature should be about $38\frac{1}{2}$°Bé, only a little thicker than it was at boiling-point.

If the syrup is too thin, it is returned to the pan and cooked a little longer. If it is too thick, a little boiling water can be stirred in. Boiling water mixes more easily with syrup than cold. It also keeps the syrup temperature up so that it is not necessary to reheat the syrup to obtain accurate hydrometer readings. When pouring or stirring this syrup, proceed very gently and certainly without any splashing, since that kind of movement encourages premature crystallising.

When the syrup has been concentrated to the correct degree, it is allowed to cool for 5 minutes or so. Then a quantity of spirit, such as brandy or rum, is tipped into the syrup, which will probably boil up as the cold liquid is added. The quantity of spirit must be exact, it should be 3 fl. oz. to each 1 lb. of sugar used to make the syrup. After adding the spirit, a damp cloth is immediately placed over the pan and a lid or plate put on top. The mixture should not be stirred at this point since this would encourage granulation, but it has to be well mixed. In fact, the boiling-up caused by the cold spirit will probably be enough to blend it in properly. The damp cloth and lid are put on to prevent any steam escaping since the steam might otherwise take quite a lot of alcohol with it. The mixture should then be allowed to cool to hand-hot, around 120°F. or so, when the liquid is still thin enough to pour easily. It can be cooled more quickly by dipping the base of the pan in cold water for a few moments. Immediately before pouring, the syrup can be stirred slowly and gently to make quite sure the spirit is fully incorporated. Liqueur syrup is poured into cornflour depressions much like fondants. Indeed, the same moulds can be used, or you can make special moulds the shape of half a bottle if you wish.

The cornflour needs a little special preparation. As a general rule, it is a good plan to run the cornflour through a wooden flour sieve occasionally to make sure any odd bits of fondant are removed. It should also be put in the oven at 100–120°F. to dry it out from time to time. Occasionally, it should be put in the oven at a higher temperature, at least 170°F. for an hour or so to make sure any bacteria which might have contaminated the cornflour are killed off. However, the oven should not be so hot that the cornflour burns.

If you are planning to use the cornflour for liqueurs, it should be dried out, although not necessarily sterilised, before using it. It can also be used while still warm. This is believed to slow down the cooling of the syrup and promote a finer crystal, although I am not sure how true this is. Nevertheless, cornflour takes impressions much more easily when warm and dry, and there is less risk of the depressions caving in as the moulds are being withdrawn. The cornflour is levelled in the starch tray and the depressions made in exactly the same way as outlined for fondants.

The syrup can be put in a small shallow saucepan with a lip and should be poured in small quantities. I find the syrup is too thin for the fondant funnel, it runs through even when the stopper is in place. The disadvantage with the saucepan is that the syrup tends to harden or crystallise at the lip, making it more difficult to pour, but it is easier with small batches. It is important to try to get the lip of the saucepan as close to the cornflour as possible so that the syrup does not have far to fall and there is less risk of the depression being put out of shape. On the other hand, this increases the risk of the base of the pan touching the surface of the cornflour and ruining the depressions. So, once again, care must be taken. It is an advantage to have a tablespoon to catch any drops from the pan as it is moved from one depression to the next.

If the syrup is too hot or too weak, it may run through the cornflour, the cornflour soaks up the syrup and when it cools it forms a hard mass. Usually this occurs, if it is going to happen at all, fairly quickly. Therefore, if three or four depressions have been filled without mishap, it is probably safe to fill the others. It is better to be sure the syrup is thick enough and cool enough. It is just as important to mix the syrup properly, even at the risk of premature graining, since if it is badly mixed, some parts are quite thick while others are much thinner and very likely to run through.

After the impressions have been filled, they should be dusted over gently with cornflour to a depth of about $\frac{1}{8}$ in. A flour dredger can be used or the cornflour put in a small sieve and shaken over the liqueurs. The purpose of this is to reduce the risk of any bacteria or yeast cells reaching the liqueurs. If too much cornflour is used carelessly, it might sink into the liqueurs and ruin them.

The liqueurs are allowed to stand for 6 to 8 hours. By this time a crystalline shell should have formed at the base of the liqueurs and to some extent up the sides, but hardly at all on the top. Therefore, they have to be turned upside down so that a shell can be encouraged to form all round. This trick, like tossing pancakes, takes a little practice. The liqueur has to be completely inverted, and it must be done with one quick flip. If the liqueur ends up at an angle, it is impossible to straighten it, it will set in a mis-shape and if you try to move it, the shell will break and the liquid be lost. A dipping fork or an ordinary household fork can be used. Also some carving forks have a gradual curve which is useful for picking the liqueurs out of the cornflour, and not too steep to cause problems when turning them over. When they are picked out, the cornflour on top of each liqueur need not be disturbed before turning it over with a quick movement of the wrist. It is possible to do this very quickly, a row at a time, with a piece of wire the same length as the row, but bent at right-angles at each end so it can be dipped into the cornflour, moved under the liqueurs and then quickly lifted to tip the liqueurs upside down.

The liqueurs should be left in the cornflour for another 6 hours at least, until they have formed a complete shell. In fact, they will take no harm if they are allowed to remain in the corn-

flour much longer. Actually, the liqueurs will not form an un-
broken shell all round for there will be a hole at the top. This
is caused because syrup contracts as it cools and part of the top
of the liqueur, being the last part to form a shell, is drawn into
the liqueur by the contraction of the interior.

Making liqueurs, like crystallising bon-bons, depends upon
the principle that sugar in solution always tends to crystallise.
If the correct concentration of sugar can be achieved, crystal-
lisation will tend to occur as the solution cools until a point is
reached where all the excess sugar has crystallised and a liquid
is left which contains only as much dissolved sugar as it is
capable of holding at room temperature. The proper quantity
of spirit added to the correct concentration of syrup gives a
mixture which crystallises out to produce a shell thick enough
for handling yet with a high concentration of spirit inside. If
the syrup were cooked to a lower degree, or if more spirit were
added, the shell would be thinner and difficult to handle. If the
syrup were made thicker, the shell would be too sugary and
unpleasant to eat. It would be possible to concentrate the syrup
further and compensate by adding more spirit but, up to a point,
the harder refined sugar is cooked, the more likely it is to
crystallise even before the spirit is added.

So far, we have discussed only straight spirits, but of course
it is possible to use liqueurs such as Benedictine, Curaçao,
Cherry Brandy and many others. However, these already contain a quantity of sugar and to add them in the same proportion
as brandy – 3 fl. oz. to 1 lb. sugar and concentrated to 38°Bé
– would produce a much higher sugar concentration and make
a much thicker sugar shell. In fact, it is quite satisfactory to add
3 fl. oz. of liqueur to 1 lb. sugar, provided the sugar syrup is
concentrated to 36°Bé. This will produce the same strength of
solution as the brandy liqueur given above. But just as beers
made by different brewers vary in their specific gravity, so
different brands of liqueur and spirit vary, and you may find it
possible to add more spirits of a particular brand, or concentrate
the syrup to a lower degree than I have recommended, and

still produce a shell strong enough to stand up to being dipped in couverture.

It would be possible to use sherry or port. These are thicker than spirits, but not as thick as liqueurs, so concentrating the sugar to 37°Bé and using the same quantities would be adequate. However, it will be found they turn out rather weak and lack the kick of spirits or liqueurs. Brandy and rum are, in fact, the thinnest liquids you are likely to use. Therefore, whatever liquid you wish to use, you will always be safe with a concentration of 38°Bé and adding 3 fl. oz. to 1 lb. of sugar. You may find a harder shell than you might wish, but it will hold together.

Dipping liqueurs also needs special care, since if one breaks and the liquid gets into the couverture this is ruined, at least for dipping; but you could use it for making truffles. First, the liqueurs have to be picked out of the cornflour and all the cornflour must be dusted off. They can be placed in a flour sieve which is then knocked gently at the side to shake the cornflour through. Then each one is lifted out and dusted with a pastry-brush and put on a clean plate or tray. You may have a little difficulty brushing out the cornflour from the hole on top, but persevere because cornflour does not improve the flavour.

The couverture should be tempered, and all the temperatures checked; the temperature of the couverture, the room and the centres, to make sure they are all correct. Also prepare a board with a sheet of silicone or wax paper to receive the dipped liqueurs. I find the best method is to dip the liqueurs twice, once by hand and the second time using a fork. The purpose of the first dipping is to strengthen the shell of the liqueur sufficiently to enable it to stand up to the second dipping, which gives it a smooth, glossy finish. Pre-bottoming is inadequate for liqueurs since they need strengthening all round.

When all is ready, put a blob of couverture on the fingers of the left hand (if right-handed) and work it between fingers and thumb. Place a liqueur on the fingers and put a little drop of couverture in the hole on top of the shell to seal it. Then work the liqueur round in the fingers to make a thin coating over the shell. To do this properly, you need just the right amount of couverture on your fingers. Too much and you get too thick a coat, too little and it does not cover the shell. If the first coat is too thick, the finished liqueur will be much less pleasant to eat since it will have a large proportion of chocolate as well as the sugar before reaching the liqueur. It is also wise to handle the liqueur well away from the bowl of tempered couverture, so that if the shell breaks, the liqueur does not get into it. When the shell is coated, it is laid out on the silicone or wax sheet to harden. It is quite likely that the couverture will set with white streaks since the temperature of your fingers may have overheated the couverture, but this is not a problem, since the liqueur is to be dipped a second time.

After the couverture has set, the liqueurs can be dipped again, using a dipping fork, and this time there is much less risk of the shell fracturing, so it is possible to do it over the bowl of couverture.

If you feel that the mixture given above, 1 lb. sugar in a solution concentrated to 38°Bé and 3fl. oz. of spirit, gives a very thick shell, it would be possible to use a little more spirit or to concentrate the syrup a little thinner, but the risk is that the shell will be more fragile. However, it would be worth leaving the liqueurs in the cornflour for a longer period of time to make sure that all the excess sugar has crystallised out of the liquid centre, thus making the shell as hard as it can be. Of course, if the syrup is too thin, there will be insufficient sugar to crystallise out and it will remain dissolved in the spirit or liqueur and not form a shell.

Having described the process of making liqueurs, it just remains to give a short summary to keep handy while you are making them.

Crystallised Brandy Liqueurs

Equipment: Two 5-in. pans, pastry-brush, thermometer, hydrometer and glass cylinder put to warm, starch tray filled with dried cornflour impressed with moulds, extra supply of warm starch, flour-dredger or sieve, damp cloth and pan lid.

Ingredients: 1 lb. granulated sugar
                 3 fl. oz. brandy.

Method: Dissolve the sugar in as little water as possible, say 4 fl. oz., and bring to the boil in accordance with the sugar-boiling procedure. When the sugar is completely dissolved, boil it quickly to 227°F. Pour enough of the boiling syrup into the warmed glass cylinder to take a hydrometer reading. It should show 38½°Bé, and you can check the temperature of the syrup in the cylinder: it should be 205–210°F. If the hydrometer reading is greater than 38½°Bé, add a little hot water and check again; if less, continue boiling the syrup. When the correct concentration has been reached, dip the base of the pan into water to check the boil, allow to cool for 5 minutes or so, then tip in the brandy. Cover with the damp cloth and lid and allow to cool to hand-hot (approximately 120°F.). If necessary, the pan can be dipped in cold water for a few moments. The syrup can then be poured into the cornflour depressions and covered with a dusting of warm starch ⅛ in. thick.

The liqueurs are turned after at least 6 hours have elapsed and they are allowed to stand for at least another 6 hours. They are removed from the cornflour, carefully sieved and dusted and given a thin coating of tempered couverture by hand and finally dipped with a fork in the usual way.

Rum or Whisky Liqueurs: These are made in the same way, using the same quantity of rum or whisky instead of brandy.

Curaçao, Benedictine, Cherry Brandy Liqueurs: As above, but concentrate the syrup to 37°Bé which is achieved at a temperature of about 226°F.

11

Presentation and Packing

Airtight containers are necessary for storing truffles in a refrigerator in order to prevent condensation forming when they
are brought out into normal temperatures, and for storing un-
wrapped caramels or nougats which attract moisture and would
otherwise become sticky. However, they are an advantage even
for other chocolates, and Woolworths sell useful boxes with
flexible blue lids which are transparent so you can see what is
inside, and which are designed to stack. The ones which measure
8 x 6 x 3½ in. will hold about three layers of chocolates, 24 to a
layer. Larger ones are an advantage if you have the storage
space. It is useful to keep a separate box for each different
centre.

Chocolates should be put into little petits-fours cases as soon
as possible after they have been dipped. Chocolates bruise easily
and the corrugated sides of the cases help to protect them.
The standard size has a diameter at the base of 1 in. and is
¾ in. deep. Some stationers stock white ones with a printed
design, but the usual chocolate-coloured ones are more difficult
to obtain. They are sold by F. G. Kettle, 127 High Holborn,
London W.C.1. and by Creeds (see p. 149). The latter also sell
gold foil cases of the same size, which are ideal for Cherry Cups.

Chocolates should be packed in boxes rather than in paper
bags, to protect them. Unfortunately, suitable chocolate boxes
are not easy to obtain in small quantities since they are usually

made only to order and in large numbers. The size has to be about right; it is irritating to put one layer in a box and find there is almost, but not quite, enough room for another layer. It is essential to measure your tallest chocolate before buying boxes. This will probably be a rose or violet cream since the crystallised decoration gives added height. Mine stand almost 1 in., therefore I have to allow 1 in. per layer and my boxes have to be either 1, 2 or 3 in. deep. As a guide, a two-layer box measuring 4 x 4 in. will probably hold about 9 oz. of chocolates, and if it measures $7\frac{1}{2}$ x 4 in. it will hold just over 1 lb.

Even professional chocolatiers find a lot of difficulty in obtaining boxes if their output is too small to justify having them made specially. When they can be found at all, they are fairly expensive. Some shops which sell greetings cards also sell attractive folding boxes which are less costly, and some large stores sometimes stock boxes towards Christmas. F. G. Kettle is, I think, the only shop in London which still sells covered boxes, including a small range of more expensive boxes which are well worth keeping even after your chocolates have been eaten. The shop also sells chocolate-coloured 'glacine' paper in sheets which is very useful for covering the bases of boxes and the top layer of chocolates. Creeds sell round boxes with transparent lids which are worth considering, although not made specially for chocolates.

In fact, it is so difficult to obtain boxes that it is well worth considering making your own. The standard rectangular covered box is not too difficult to make: you could buy one from Kettle's to serve as a model. The materials you will need are a suitable weight of cardboard and 'glacine' paper to line it, or 'glacine-backed board' if you can get it; patterned or gold paper to decorate the cover – Kettles' stock a range; clear adhesive Bostik or a similar glue; a little sellotape to stick the corners of the box together temporarily until the lining paper can be put on; a Stanley knife and a ruler, preferably made of steel.

Another idea is to buy small decorated bowls or plates, fill them with chocolates and cover with cellophane. Scallop shells can be filled the same way. The appearance of any container is enormously enhanced if finished off with a gaily-coloured ribbon tied in a bow, not one of those manufactured ones which are stuck on. For a large bow which holds its shape, you will need ribbon wired along both edges.

A thin piece of cardboard between layers of chocolate gives a firm base to the upper layer and prevents damage to the lower one. White cardboard can be obtained from artists' suppliers and can be cut to size. Chocolate-coloured cardboard or 'glacine-backed board' is much better but extremely difficult to obtain in small quantities. It can be obtained from Mitcham Cardboard Ltd., 99 Beddington Lane, Croydon, Surrey, but has to be collected.

Foil is extremely useful for wrapping liqueurs as a warning that the centre is very liquid, but it seems to be impossible to buy in small quantities, partly because it is so fragile. I can only suggest that a professional chocolatier may perhaps be able to let you have some.

Index

Index

Index